THE LITTLE BOOK

—— OF ——

WELLNESS

*An A–Z guide to nourish body,
mind + soul*

TRACY RICHARDSON

DEDICATION

For Mum, Dad, Russ, Sarah, Raven, Barley and Pickles –
helping to nourish my body, mind + soul.

CONTENTS

INTRODUCTION

'The moment you take responsibility for everything in your life is the moment you can change anything in your life.'

Hal Elrod.

Wellness is the opposite of illness and is essentially what makes you a 'well being'.

Wellness encompasses the choices you make, the environments you are in, the people you associate with, the thoughts you have, the lifestyle you lead, and the foods you consume. All of these factors, plus much more, directly influence the state of your holistic health.

So you could say wellness is the nourishment of your body, your mind and your soul.

In writing this book, I wanted to reach out to as many people as possible and discuss wellness from a practical point of view, backed up with research, as something achievable that can be easily developed through daily practices and that you have a great deal of influence upon. I want to promote wellness as something you have choices about and for which there are so many things you can do to take control of – something you become actively involved in to be your own wellness advocate in support of your own and your family's wellness.

Wellness is something I have contemplated writing about for a few years and have been actively working on my whole life through the experiences, evidence-based practice, and formal training and education I have encountered.

> *'When we strive to become better than we are, everything around us becomes better too.'*
>
> **Paul Coelho.**

So why an A to Z?

Oftentimes it is really hard to take on board lots of information at once, especially when it is new material, and then to absorb and translate it into direct actions that culminate in changes to your lifestyle. It can be overwhelming and off-putting from the start. But, by having an easy to refer to, reference-style A to Z book with keywords you'll be able to work through at your own pace, dip in and out of, and check back easily at any point, I hope this book becomes a source of encouragement to support you on your wellness journey.

> *'A journey of a thousand miles begins with a single step.'*
>
> **Lao Tzu.**

I hope this book speaks to you in the same way I've written it to reflect my unique style of in-person client consultations.

> *If you wish for wellness, you need to be willing to remove the reasons for your illness*
>
> **~ Tracy Richardson.**

* Please note this book is for informational purposes only and is not designed in any way to be prescriptive, or to replace a doctor's or physician's advice, but may act as a bridge between the patient and the doctor. The information contained should not be construed as medical advice. Before embarking upon any changes to lifestyle, a physician or primary caregiver should be consulted. This book offers information about self-care and promotes understanding about the body and how you may support it.

A – ANTIOXIDANTS

This chapter will help you if you:

> Want to learn about the importance of antioxidants

> Want to learn about the influence of oxidative stress on your wellness

> Want top tips on how to boost antioxidants and reduce oxidative stress.

You may have heard of antioxidants. It's certainly a buzzword with regards to nutrition, but what are they?

Antioxidants are substances that work to prevent cellular damage from the free radicals you produce. When you break things down using oxygen (a totally normal process), this is called oxidation, and it is how you turn your food into energy for the body. It also produces free radicals. Free radicals are unpaired and unstable electrons that scavenge in the body to find a free electron to stabilise themselves. This may wreak havoc in the body when the terrain of a person is less than optimal. An antioxidant will donate an electron to neutralise the free radical in order to prevent their build-up and reduce oxidative stress on the body. When you have enough antioxidants, your body functions effectively and you are well.

When the production of free radicals outweighs the antioxidant availability, this becomes an issue. If you don't possess the resources to deal with free radicals, the body is under oxidative stress and you manifest this as unwanted symptoms like pain and inflammation. Free radicals are indiscriminate as to where they scavenge electrons from and often steal them from healthy cells. Free radicals are not all bad; however, they become a concern when there are too many for too long a time as they can damage cells' lipid (fat) walls, proteins and DNA molecules.

Antioxidants are essential for life in more ways than you may realise. Excessive stress on the body systems depletes antioxidants, and so the demand far outweighs the supply. If you are chronically exposed to stressors, such as toxins from the environment, a crappy diet, strong medications, chronic stress, and physical or emotional trauma or illness, then your antioxidant levels are likely depleted. In fact, the older you are, the more depleted they become.

The following are some of the main antioxidants.

The master antioxidant is glutathione as it can recycle itself. It consists of three amino acids – cysteine, glycine and glutamine – and is found in most body tissues but mainly the liver, an organ that is continuously slammed by oxidative stress. Glutathione is a key antioxidant and detoxifying agent as it neutralises free radicals, supports the immune system, is the main antioxidant in the brain, reduces cortisol, supports sleep quality and slows cellular ageing. Glutathione is found in foods like garlic, broccoli, asparagus, avocado, cabbage, Brussel sprouts, spinach, chives, tomatoes, cucumber and nuts like almonds and walnuts. Drinking bone broth or consuming gelatine and collagen are excellent ways to supply the necessary amino acids to form glutathione. You should also be working on gut health and better digestion (check out chapters D – Detoxing, N – Nutrients and Z – Zzzz: sleep for support with this).

Melatonin increases the ability of glutathione to scavenge free radicals, promotes glutathione recycling and maintains levels of glutathione as an antioxidant. Without melatonin, you have no glutathione. Melatonin is produced in the pineal gland and by the mitochondria in your cells and is five times stronger than glutathione, supporting sleep quality, cellular regeneration, the immune system, fertility and the coordination of many processes in the body (see Chapter C – Circadian rhythms for more details on melatonin).

Carnosine is one of your primary antioxidants, formed from the amino acids alanine and histidine, and is known as the body's anabolic steroid (helps to build tissue). It is regulated by the pituitary gland and supports hormonal management. Carnosine protects protein structures from damage, helps to protect your mitochondria (where you produce energy) from free radicals and supports cell function. It is great for your skin, organs, nerves and connective tissue and helps to remove lactic acid. Carnosine is primarily found in meat, poultry and fish.

Nitric oxide has many roles and can also be considered an antioxidant. It is naturally occurring in the body in our endothelial cells lining the blood vessels and supports blood circulation and oxygenation by acting as a vasodilator to enhance blood flow. Nitric oxide has a role in pain relief, cellular renewal, white blood cell function, bone formation and energy production (see Chapter B – Breathing) and is apparently boosted by beetroot!

Humic and fulvic acids are well known as highly beneficial and powerful antioxidants. The fulvic–humic complex has a unique ability to support chemical balance and can either act as a donor or electron acceptor to neutralise harmful free radicals (see more in Chapter N – Nutrients). Although we should be able to get these antioxidants from our natural food sources, years of over farming and chemical use have depleted nutrients in the soil and they are no longer passed on to the plant life; instead, you can supplement in the form of fulvic-humic powder.

Vitamin C is the primary circulatory antioxidant in the blood plasma and so acts to spare other internal antioxidants. The brain, brainstem and adrenal glands contain more internally produced stores of vitamin C than any other body tissue. Only after vitamin C is used up is glutathione utilised. Whole food or external sources of vitamin C are found in foods like citrus fruits, blackcurrants, strawberries, kiwis, bell peppers and broccoli.

The main fat-soluble antioxidant is vitamin E, which has a vital role in protecting cell membranes from free radical damage. It is found in nuts and seeds, some vegetables and fruits (such as avocado, red sweet pepper, mango and apricots) and oily fish like salmon and trout.

Selenium also works as an antioxidant, and some studies state that it can help balance hormones and support thyroid function. It is found in brazil nuts, mushrooms, free-range organic eggs, spinach and raw cheeses made from goat's, sheep's and A2 cow's milk (Jersey cows).

Antioxidants are mostly found in colourful fruits and vegetables. '*Foods that are deep blue, purple, red, green, or orange are leaders in antioxidants and contain many nutrients that boost immunity and enhance health.*' Deepak Chopra.

If you are chronically exposed to toxins from the environment, a poor diet, strong medications, excessive stress or physical or emotional trauma or illness, then your antioxidant levels are likely depleted. As you age, the more depleted your levels become. To support your wellness and ensure that you are not accumulating more free radicals than your body can manage, aim to consume wholesome nutrient-dense foods, reduce your exposure to toxins in the environment and the home, and reduce both your external and internal (self-imposed) stress.

Free radicals are present in the development of dis-ease (a state opposite to ease) and dysfunction in the body. Thus, consuming quality fruits and vegetables full of phytonutrients and antioxidants supports combatting free radicals and oxidative stress. A healthy diet is more beneficial than synthetic pill and capsule supplements, which are at best broken down and degraded by digestion, though sometimes are necessary; however, you may be able to support yourself via other holistic means.

You can make changes to your lifestyle – eat better, move more and eliminate or reduce stressors. Where possible, grow your fruit and vegetables or select organic. Always be aware of where your food comes from and what you're putting into your temple!

If you eat a healthy, organic, nutrient-dense and balanced diet containing fruits and vegetables, you are already getting lots of antioxidants and supporting your wellness.

'Let food be thy medicine and let medicine be thy food.'

Hippocrates.

TOP TIPS

➤ Make your meals colourful and try to have fruits and/or vegetables with every meal.

➤ Consume nutrient-dense foods – organic, seasonal and local. Grow your own if you can.

➤ Where you require support, consider humic–fulvic acid to replace the nutrients lost from depleted soils and foodstuffs (see Chapter N – Nutrients).

➤ Supplement only when necessary. Supplements should never be used in place of a nutrient-dense diet as they can affect the natural feedback mechanisms in cells, so it is best to support natural processes. Consider homeopathy, herbs and frequency medicine under the guidance of a qualified practitioner (see Chapter E – Energy).

➤ Utilise time and techniques to help you relax and recharge your body, mind and soul (see Chapter U – Unwind).

B – BREATHING

This chapter will help you if you:

> ➤ Want to know the importance and effects of breathing well
> ➤ Want to know how to identify your breathing style
> ➤ Want top tips on how to practise breathing correctly.

When was the last time somebody told you to 'shut your mouth'?

It's probably been a while and it's not very polite, but it's one of the most important things you can do to improve your health.

Let me explain. Breathing is the process of taking air into the lungs and expelling it back out. However, a fundamental element of breathing is the nasal breath. If you think about it, the nose was designed for breathing, whilst the mouth was designed for talking and eating.

Mouth breathing has its place when you're exerting yourself as it helps to get air in quickly. But it's not an effective or efficient long-term strategy and can even lead to problems.

When you breathe through your mouth, it alerts your brain that the body is under stress and stimulates 'fight or flight' mode, activating the sympathetic nervous system (SNS) branch of the autonomic nervous system (ANS) which prepares you for action. This all happens at an involuntary level that you are not in conscious control over. If you breathe through your mouth regularly, your brain thinks it's under threat and your innate survival instincts kick in. Your nervous system is over sensitised, which can lead to exhaustion of the body's systems.

Mouth breathing can lead to you over-breathing (yes, it's a thing), upper thoracic breathing (stress breathing), snoring (boo) and sleep apnoea. It also gives off 42% more water, so you become more dehydrated. The mouth should be closed, the tongue should rest on the roof of the mouth behind the top teeth in a relaxed position, and you should breathe into the diaphragm to allow your lungs to expand.

'80% of the population is not breathing correctly.' Alan Dolan.

So, how do you know if you're breathing correctly?

If you have nasal congestion, allergies, a persistent dry throat and/or cough, sleep apnoea, grind your teeth or have high levels of anxiety, you may have a dysfunctional way of breathing.

If you are a habitual mouth breather, you are likely a chest breather also and the shallow breaths you take indicate stressful breathing to the brain. You can check if you are a shallow chest breather by placing one hand on your chest and the other hand on your tummy. When you breathe, notice which hand moves first. If it is the upper hand, then the diaphragm and respiratory muscles are not working effectively. You can try this when you are walking around as well and the effect may be more noticeable.

Diaphragmatic breathing is often indicated by practitioners. The diaphragm is a muscle located in the centre of your chest and spans the lower rib cage. When you inhale, the air enters the nose, travels down the throat and into the lungs. As the lungs fill, the diaphragm contracts and drops down, the organs move down gently, the belly expands and the pelvic floor expands. This creates a vacuum that draws air into your lungs. The lungs fill in 360 degrees as the chest expands outwards to increase the breathing volume of the abdomen. Upon exhaling, the reverse pattern occurs where the muscles of the pelvic floor and diaphragm move up, and the breath moves out of the lungs from the bottom to the top.

Nasal breathing is efficient breathing and promotes an upright spinal posture, providing a clear airway into the lungs. This type of breathing creates a sensation of lightness in the body and calm in the mind.

The nose acts to filter, warm and moisten the air you breathe in; the mouth doesn't do this, which can mean that toxins and bacteria bypass this part of your defence system. Nasal breathing supports diaphragmatic breathing by taking the air deeper into the lungs. This is a non-stressful breath and activates the parasympathetic nervous system (PNS) causing a relative response. In turn, diaphragmatic breathing can increase melatonin whilst decreasing cortisol, free radicals and oxidative stress.

Nasal breathing increases the resistance to airflow by around 50%, which results in a 10–20% increase in oxygen uptake. Nitric oxide is produced in the nasal cavity, which acts to dilate the airways and blood vessels, so more oxygen can be exchanged and absorbed into the bloodstream. However, it is the exhale that is key to your oxygen saturation, as when you breathe out, this signals the body as to the carbon dioxide levels present and cues that you need to inhale.

Dr Buteyko, who developed the Buteyko method of breathwork in the 1950s, indicated that healthy people have quiet, effortless nasal breathing at rest; through practising nasal breathing during the daytime, this becomes more commonplace at night, and nasal breathing during your sleep is really important. Plus, your dentist will love you as it reduces the incidence of cavities, malocclusion (misaligned teeth) and periodontitis (gum disease). The Buteyko method encourages mouth taping at night to ensure nasal breathing. However, this may come with its own set of caveats and contraindications.

Becoming aware of your breath and breathing mindfully can help you to optimise your breath and promote health. Did you know you only ever breathe through one nostril at a time, and this changes every 30–60 minutes? Nasal breathing helps soothe the nervous system and promotes relaxation and calm. Imagine inhaling the feeling of calm and exhaling the feeling of worry. Remember that the present is a gift, stay in the moment and breathe through it.

Whenever you find yourself overly stressed, focus on your breath, specifically the air as it flows in and out through the nostrils. Become conscious of the breath. Follow it while it flows in and out of your lungs as the chest expands and relaxes and focus on the process of breathing. Then take a brief pause after each inhalation and exhalation. Within a few moments, you will begin to physically relax and unwind. You may not be able to change your situation, but this process will allow you to alter your response to it by allowing your mind to settle through conscious breathing. Calm the body and the mind will follow.

'Breathe in deeply to bring your mind home to your body.'

Thich Nhat Hanh.

TOP TIPS

Firstly, pick a comfortable position – you need to practise breathing!

➤ Close your mouth for nasal breathing and try ten breaths in and out through your nose.

➤ Next, you can progress onto diaphragmatic breathing. Place your hands on your abdomen, just beneath the rib cage, and take a breath in. Imagine there is a balloon in your tummy and, on each in-breath, you are inflating that balloon 360 degrees. Feel this area expand gently as you breathe in and fall back into place as you breathe out. You are trying to get the diaphragm muscle to contract and relax.

➤ The lower ribs should feel like they're moving sideways and outwards as you inhale and then feel like they're moving back down as you exhale. It is not a 'deep breath' so the movement is only small. On the out-breath, the air is released and the balloon deflated – just let it go (all through the nose).

➤ Now, try ten breaths of box breathing – in for four counts, hold for four counts, out for four counts and hold for four counts.

C – CIRCADIAN RHYTHMS

This chapter will help you if you:

➢ Want to know what circadian rhythms are

➢ Want to know how light and dark affects your wellness

➢ Want Top Tips on how to support your circadian rhythms.

Circadian rhythm is the synchronisation of the body processes with the environment – specifically light frequencies from the sun and the earth's magnetic field – via receptors in the eyes and skin. They sense both the presence and absence of light frequencies and tell the master clock in the brain what time of day it is.

> *'We have made clocks that are perfectly in sync with the industrial machinery and the information age and perfectly out of sync with nature and our circadian rhythm.'*
> **Khang Kijarro Nguyen.**

So how does this happen? Essentially, ultraviolet (UV) light interacts with receptors in the eyes and skin and with the amino acid tryptophan, which is then converted into serotonin. This serotonin is stored in the gut where it is released at night, and the pineal gland converts this into melatonin. The pineal gland in the brain releases melatonin when there is no light present and peaks four hours after darkness. Melatonin is turned down or even off by any light exposure after sunset.

Melatonin is really important. It not only has a huge role in preparing the body for sleep, but it also supports aerobic energy production and cellular renewal processes, acts as an antioxidant and scavenges for free radicals (see Chapter A – Antioxidants). Thus, melatonin protects your body tissues, especially cell membranes and DNA, and also boosts the effectiveness of another antioxidant, glutathione, the master antioxidant. Additionally, melatonin has a huge role in fertility and the immune system as it is present in every cell.

You need adequate daily sunlight (full spectrum light) and darkness for adequate melatonin production. This only occurs when the receptors in the eye don't detect blue light and when the gut isn't digesting food. If the light–dark cycle is affected, and you never get to the point where you are in total darkness, or 'fasted', the body cannot work effectively to release melatonin. So, if you have eaten a large meal just before bed, or if you have lots of blue light coming into your eyes and onto your skin from technology like phones and TV screens, this doesn't happen. Not only is your sleep disrupted but many other processes are also affected which can lead to an array of dysfunctions that manifest as symptoms such as fatigue, insomnia and dehydration.

Melatonin also influences the digestion of foods relative to the time of day. So how does this affect your Christmas? Have you ever wondered why you get sleepy after Christmas day lunch? Well, melatonin is a derivative of the amino acid tryptophan and turkey is filled with tryptophan.

Being exposed to blue light at the wrong times and over long periods is similar to consuming excessive carbohydrates over a long period – it alters mitochondrial function in your cells and hence energy production and use. Mitochondria are accustomed to seasonal variation, and overexposure to blue light disrupts energy production and body function. Life is all about energy generation, which happens in the mitochondria, and energy utilisation. So, just like the engine in a Ferrari, the mitochondria need to be efficient for you to remain well.

Light temperature is measured in kelvins from 1000K to 10,000K, though most lighting is between 2000K to 6500K, with daylight around 6500K. The blue hue from artificial light fools your eyes into believing it is midday or solar noon, so if the time is 9 pm, this disrupts your circadian rhythm. Additionally, the body cannot release serotonin from the gut if it is busy digesting, and if there is light present, the melatonin is not released.

When you wake in response to light, your cortisol levels should be high to provide the impetus to get you going in the morning, peaking between 6 and 9 am when melatonin is naturally lower. If you avoid morning sunlight or have too much artificial light at night, your light environment is disrupted and so are your body processes.

Light affects your hormones, your sleep–wake cycles, food intake, mood, energy production and the immune system. Dark influences melatonin production, sleep, detoxification processes and cellular regeneration. Every gene is linked to a 'clock' that is controlled by light and the absence of light.

Light affects life. Light is life.

Having bright lights, gadgets and the TV at the touch of a switch means it is so easy for your circadian rhythm to become disrupted. An altered sleep–wake pattern can also lead to fatiguing the adrenal glands where exposure to chronic stress or artificial light at night (ALAN) causes the adrenal glands to produce more cortisol without allowing the adrenals to rest and recover.

Artificial light does not resemble sunlight; it does not have the appropriate combination of light frequencies and has very high levels of blue and green, which promote wakefulness, and their absence promotes sleep. This acts to disrupt your natural circadian rhythm and has a knock-on effect upon many processes, including metabolism, sleep, hormone production and fertility. Exposing your eyes and skin to artificial light lowers melatonin, which impairs the mitochondrial ability to make the intracellular water you need to make vitamin D. This also impairs the 100Hz cellular frequency needed by mitochondria for fat burning during sleep.

Going to bed after midnight also means you have already missed out on two hours' worth of your innate physical repair cycle, which starts around 10 pm. Over time, this can lead to lots of low-level symptomatic complaints like muscle aches, headaches and low mood. You can train your body to develop dysfunctional patterns where the hormones and processes become dysregulated, so a night-time routine is essential to promote rest and rejuvenation.

This is not the whole story, but supporting your circadian rhythms is an easy way for you to enhance your health. Your lifestyle and your environment are individual to you (n=1), and they have a huge influence on your cells and their function. You need to make optimal choices so that you can enjoy optimal wellness.

TOP TIPS

➤ Consider your light environment. Use a filter on your tech and screens – check out iris, or wear blue-blocking glasses after sundown if you are using artificial light.

➤ Don't eat after dark where possible. This will help to support natural sleep, hormone balance and serotonin release!

➤ Try to see the sunrise and the sunset every day; this helps to reset the clock in your brain.

➤ Develop a night-time routine that supports sleep (see Chapter Z – Zzzz: sleep).

D – DETOXING

This chapter will help you if you

➤ Want to know how your body detoxes

➤ Want to know the signs to look for when your body needs help

➤ Want Top Tips on how to support your body's detox processes.

> *'If you don't take care of this the most magnificent machine that you will ever be given... where are you going to live?'*

> **Karyn Calabrese.**

Detoxing may not be what you think it is.

Your body is detoxing you all the time. A detox is not a 'diet' or a 'regime' that you embark upon; it is a detoxification process within the body that is naturally occurring and promotes the harmonious functioning of your body systems.

Every cell in your body has a detoxification system or a drainage/ excretion system. It is a process of normal operations where the cell is cleansing itself – not an external strategy. You can, however, choose to support these processes – especially if they have become inefficient and stagnated – with nutrition, hydration, breathwork, movement and some therapies. Most people need only a gentle approach that supports their organ systems through natural actions in an otherwise overburdened body, much like cleaning a polluted fish tank.

For your body to effectively go through its detoxification activity, a series of chemical reactions must occur consisting of reduction and oxidation in the mitochondria of your cells, which is known as redox. This is where the energy is produced to ensure your cells, organs and body systems are functioning effectively, so it is important to promote cell health.

You need a high level of redox for your cells to undergo protein synthesis for restoration, regeneration and renewal. One indicator that your redox potential is up to par is dreaming as this indicates your cell membranes contain a lot of stored energy (charge). Additionally, skin, hair and nails that have good condition indicate a good level of redox. If you feel that your redox needs a boost, then here are some ways you can support yourself: no alcohol, reduced exposure to toxins in household items and personal care products, grounding (see Chapter G – Grounding), drinking good quality water (see Chapter W – Water) and lowering your stress levels.

Your body is always working to detoxify your system; it is super smart and knows what it does and doesn't need. Your main detox organs are the lungs, liver, gut, kidneys and skin along with the lymphatic system. Unfortunately, they often bear the brunt of your lifestyle decisions and dietary choices. This is how you should think about detoxification – as a series of processes to remove what is not serving you.

Your liver has over 500 roles in the body. It detoxes you by changing fat-soluble toxins to water-soluble toxins so they can be easily flushed out of your system. This has two stages and requires many factors.

The first stage requires lots of B vitamins and glutathione to facilitate this process. The second stage needs B vitamins, glutathione, magnesium and amino acids.

Your kidneys act as a filtration system and help to regulate your body's pH, electrolytes and detoxification. Once the toxins are filtered, the kidneys allow them to be flushed out in your urine.

Your skin is semipermeable and the largest organ in the body, so it is an easy way to get rid of toxins through sweating and often as skin conditions; it's not just about cooling down.

Your digestive system and your gastrointestinal tract (GI) are together a huge way to detoxify you when all is running smoothly! If you suffer from constipation, then this is causing toxins to build up in the system.

Your lungs help too. Every time you exhale, you are breathing out the gases that the body cannot utilise, namely nitrogen and carbon dioxide, but you are also excreting toxins.

You have a continuous flow of toxins from your cells and organs. So if any part of the process is inefficient, overburdened or ineffective and not flowing/moving, then your whole system develops congestion or stagnation. This leads to a build-up of toxicity. Your body undergoes oxidative stress (see Chapter A – Antioxidants) if the production of free radicals outweighs the resources to neutralise them, and issues start to occur. The inconvenient symptoms that you dismiss are in fact warning signals from your body.

The lymphatic system is probably the most neglected in the body because most people don't even know it exists, though it should be at the forefront of your mind when it comes to wellness. It's essentially the cellular waste disposal system. Think of it as the internal sewage system for the waste produced naturally by our cells (digestion). It also distributes your white blood cells and therefore plays a huge part in your immune defence. But it can become overloaded so rather than removing toxins and waste, it becomes congested and a bit like a toxic soup.

The lymphatic system is comprised of billions of lymph capillaries, over 700 lymph nodes and approximately 15 litres of lymph fluid that needs to circulate throughout the body. If this can't flow, you've got problems. Your cells are only as healthy as the environment they live in, so if the lymphatic system is unable to sort through the nutrients and cellular waste, it is not directed to the relevant detoxification pathways and elimination organs. The lymphatic system has no pump and moves in response to changes in pressure as you move and breathe.

By continually adding to this load, the lymphatics become congested, which in turn influences all of your body's functions. You then can't remove the waste effectively; what you don't eliminate, you accumulate.

This waste builds up. It's acidic in nature and lowers the pH in the surrounding cells. What does acid do? It burns. This creates massive amounts of free radicals, oxidative stress and inflammation in the body which has nowhere to go. Without the resources to remove waste or deliver nutrients and antioxidants, oxygen becomes insufficient and your cells become suffocated and damaged by their own debris, causing dysfunction and dis-ease.

You undoubtedly will experience symptoms that indicate your detoxification processes are under stress. If your digestion is sluggish and toxins remain in the gut for too long, you experience inefficient waste removal and/or constipation as the bowels are not moving waste out, which can mean toxins back up into the lymph fluid and blood. This may then alternate with reduced nutrient absorption from diarrhoea in which case the bowel has toxicity and is trying to flush itself. Your gut is under constant assault; so when it is overwhelmed, it simply cannot function 'normally'. This may also affect your mood (via the gut–brain link).

If your body is overloaded with toxins, everything feels sluggish and slower. You may feel bloated and the weight is creeping up despite your best efforts. Lots of toxicity in the body can lead to unexpected weight gain and congestion, so if you've taken steps to lose weight and still had no luck, a lifestyle check-in may be necessary to determine the best course of action. Lack of activity, imbalanced gut bacteria, lifestyle choices, environmental toxins and eating habits are amongst the things that influence your weight.

When your lymphatic system is not functioning optimally, it can lead to an overload of other detox organs and body systems. It can also result in an increased production of bodily fat. Fats/lipids are transported in your lymphatic system and too many can make the lymph flow sluggish. By ensuring your lymphatic system is functioning well, you are giving your body a much better chance and maintaining wellness.

Another common sign your body has too many built-up toxins is skin issues, all of which are frustrating to deal with and can seriously affect your mental wellness. The skin is considered the third kidney in Traditional Chinese Medicine (TCM), so many skin issues relate to an overloaded system and poor filtration in the liver, gut and kidneys (body hierarchy). Because the skin is the largest organ, issues here are one of the first areas to indicate that something is going on as the body looks to excrete what it can via the route of least resistance.

Getting eight hours of sleep a night and still feeling tired is a sign of an overloaded system. The body is not working efficiently, or maybe it just doesn't possess the energy and resources it requires to combat oxidative stress and maintain equilibrium. Insomnia, or waking between 1 and 3 am (liver o'clock in TCM), relates to an overburdened liver.

If your fatigue is caused by accumulated toxins in your body, your energy is being used up to try and deal with the toxin backlog. The go-to 'fatigue fixes' like caffeine don't change anything and you will still feel completely drained. Feeling tired affects nearly every aspect of your life, but if you're not addressing the root cause, it will persist. The result is often brain fog from the congestion in the blood and lymphatic fluid and impeded filtration via the liver and kidneys.

One of the ways your body tries to detoxify is through producing mucous as an immune response to trap and remove pathogens and other potentially harmful substances. However, you don't often realise you are sabotaging yourself as many foods you consume create acid – think processed foods – and are mucous forming. The body uses its response system to reduce this acidity so the body can continue to function well. If all your body systems are working effectively, then acid is simply removed and that's that. But, if your detoxification or elimination systems are dysfunctional, then the mucous accumulates.

What can you do to support your body's detoxification process?

If your body systems are 'backed up', then it is wise to get them moving. You should have at least one bowel movement a day so if you are constipated, then firstly look at your hydration and food intake. Drinking more water and avoiding coffee and alcohol help, along with short-term supplementation of magnesium gluconate as it irritates the gut and promotes movement. Diarrhoea means poor nutrient absorption in the gut, though binders like zeolite, clay and charcoal may also be options to help remove toxins and prevent disruption to the gut and bowels. However, consulting with an appropriate holistic health practitioner is a wise move as the root cause should always be addressed.

If there are disruptions to the gut, then the liver is overburdened and the production and flow of bile from the gall bladder is also affected.

Bile helps with the digestion of fats and pathogen elimination, so when this is impeded, toxins may return to the blood circulation. So supporting the liver is essential. Again, consulting a practitioner is the best option here.

There are numerous 'detox plans' out there, but dumping your stored toxins into a stagnant system is akin to adding more rubbish into an already overflowing bin. If you undergo an induced detox process and your wellness seems to worsen as the toxins become mobilised, they are being redistributed into the system that is already overloaded. So supporting your body processes is the first port of call.

As your body undergoes detox, you may experience some unwanted symptoms, though it is simply your body removing what is not serving it. Some signs that your system is detoxing include an increase in mucous, mild fever and chills, headaches (linked to the gut which starts to drain as the bowels clear), hair loss (old, weak cells leaving is natural), itching (the skin will expel what the kidneys cannot), gas and bloating, constipation or diarrhoea and general aches (acids being released into tissues curating temporary stiffness). Increase your fluid intake and rest when possible.

How long will it take? How much effort will you need? No one can tell you; it is all about how receptive your body is and the state of the body's terrain. If you don't feel that you can go it alone, take it one step at a time, reach out and get support, follow up for accountability and allow your body to heal.

You are healthful and vitalised beings of light. By taking a holistic view and ensuring that you work with the body and not against it, you can move towards wellness restoration and maintenance. Listening to your body – and providing it with the energy and resources it needs – you can trust in your body's ability to heal. Remember – healing takes time.

Looking for ways to reduce the amount of work your body needs to do means there is more energy and resources for wellness. Most things can be absorbed into your blood and tissues, creating a toxic overload in your body, so reducing anything processed can support your healing.

Are you ready to let go of what is not serving you? The food, the relationships, the habits and behaviours? Simplicity – can you handle it?

It all starts with the first step.

TOP TIPS

➤ Increase your water intake. It sounds basic, but if you are dehydrated, then your stools may be harder to pass! Hydration is essential to restoring lymphatic and kidney function and to move out the congested lymphatic waste.

➤ Increase your consumption of fruit and veggies whilst decreasing your consumption of processed foods, proteins and fats. The increased nutrients and water content will help improve the digestive process. If you struggle with this, try juicing! This stimulates your organs and body systems to start moving.

➤ Ensure that your diet is filled with nutrients (see Chapter N – Nutrients) and not filled with supplements, though you may consider taking humic-fulvic acid, organic greens and/or liquid zeolite to help chelate and remove toxins from the system once the bowels are working better.

➤ Reduce or remove harmful chemicals from the home and personal care products to reduce your toxic load. Consider essential oils instead of perfume (my personal favourite is dōTerra On Guard), use aluminium-free deodorant and hair-care products that are SLS, EDTA and paraben free (also check the water source); try rosehip oil or coconut oil for the skin. Not only will these options help your skin to detox by unclogging pores, but they also reduce the toxic load on the lymphatics.

➢ Reduce your stress and aim for existing in a tranquil environment.

➢ Red light therapy can be helpful in cases of leaky gut because of the link between serotonin and melatonin in the small bowel.

➢ Get moving. This supports sweating (excretion), lymph flow, blood circulation, waste removal and nutrient delivery. There is no pump in the lymphatic system so it relies on muscle contraction to stimulate flow. You can also try diaphragmatic breathing (see Chapter B – Breathing). You are designed to move – not to sit for hours a day.

➢ Your skin is your biggest detox organ. A warm bath with Epsom salts is a fabulous way to support detox as sweating is one of your body's detox routes and the skin is known as the third kidney (a detox organ), which helps to create mucous for better excretion.

E – ENERGY

This chapter will help you if you:

➢ Want to know how energy and frequencies affect you

➢ Want to know how you can sense energy

➢ Want Top Tips on how to support your energy and frequencies.

It's true when you hear it said: 'It's all about the good vibrations.' Or frequencies, resonance, energy … whatever you want to call it.

> *'Energy cannot be created or destroyed; it can only*
> *be changed from one form to another.'*
> **Albert Einstein.**

So, in other words, energy doesn't dissipate; it simply changes its configuration.

Consider that everything is energy and that you are a being of vibrational energy that resonates at different frequencies.

You can see frequencies being measured with an electrocardiogram (ECG), developed in 1887, that records electrical activity in the heart and also with an electroencephalogram (EEG), developed in 1875, that records electrical activity in the brain. These frequencies are transmitted through your nervous system where your nerve cells or neurons replicate the frequency of the nerve cells next to them; think fibre optic cables for the internet. The frequency conveyed is determined by the interactions of the neurons.

You could say that you are electric as you are governed by the electrical signals throughout the nervous system. There are millions of different bioelectrical frequencies running through you right now. Your central nervous system (CNS) is like a huge network that directs signals to create fusions, influence your biochemistry and produce many molecules, ions and enzymes that allow your body to function.

All of your body structures have different frequencies and many areas have multiple frequencies. Bone has 14 to 19 resonant frequencies, is not solid and has a crystalline structure so bone has piezoelectric properties – an electric charge in response to mechanical loading. You can stimulate the bone to improve the flow of energy through tapping on areas such as the top of your head, the inner edge of your eyebrow, under your eye on the cheekbone or the side of the hand, though you can tap on any bone. The frequencies are determined by the wave and spin of atoms that make up the matter in the body. If you break it all down, you are a tightly packed, highly attracted bundle of atoms that is spinning super fast.

Bioelectricity is based on the electron transport or ionic flow of positively charged ions like potassium, sodium and calcium. You can note this happening in muscle contractions, your heartbeat and in the signalling of your nervous system. Every thought, movement and feeling you have are all controlled by bioelectricity.

Your CNS is like a giant antenna for this type of energy. Your cells respond to specific frequencies much like the antenna for your TV.

Receptors in the cells or antennae resonate and vibrate at a specific frequency; when a signal resonates with the antenna, the signal tunes in and creates a TV picture or, in the cells, a biophysical response.

Have you ever been around someone and felt good vibes or bad vibes? Then you have already experienced frequencies for yourself. This is your antennae reading their frequency! It's *your* frequencies interpreting and tuning into *their* frequencies. You could look at it as a self-preservation mechanism or a sixth sense.

The things you encounter daily affect your vibrational frequency and influence your energy, possibly in more ways than you realise. You are highly affected by the people around you via their energy fields. Your energy field extends outwards around two metres, though can extend much further. The quantum field is an invisible field of frequency and energy that connects everything. You are surrounded by your energy field – a natural energy flow that is essential for optimal wellness.

Think about how you feel around the people in your life. There are energy radiators and energy drains out there, and you indeed become what you are surrounded by. Have you ever walked into a room and sensed that it was full of 'good vibes' and you wanted to stay? Or been around someone and felt physically drained after a conversation with them? When you are around those vibrating at a lower resonance or lower energy than yours, you can feel drained of energy and not able to reach your potential. So, take notice of when you are around people who are radiators vibrating at a higher resonance. You become a vibrant being too who feels awesome.

Each vibration is equivalent to a feeling and in the 'vibrational' world, there are only two kinds of vibrations, positive and negative. Thus, any feeling causes you to emit a vibration which can be positive or negative.

Just like with electricity in your home, through your nervous system, you can experience resistance in the bioelectrical currents of the body. This disrupts your cellular function and you can experience various symptoms like pain and inflammation. It's your body's response to a weak, faulty or interrupted signal. When these signals are interrupted, weakened or in some way damaged, stress is created within the system which then compensates. For example, a heel injury causing pain can result in an altered gait pattern. Energy flow is influenced by trauma, both emotional and physical, which affects your wellness.

Your brain cells are loaded with docosahexaenoic acid (DHA), which changes electrical and magnetic signals to chemical signals and uses water to convert these to energy.

So the body is not just biology and chemistry, it's physics too. Any type of stress causes a loss of DHA in your cell membranes. Depending on the trauma or problem, you will observe the effects in your neurons, gut and mitochondria.

When the body doesn't have the energy and resources to deal with physical, mental or emotional trauma, you become symptomatic and this manifests as dysfunction or dis-ease. If you feel like you have low energy, it means you're losing the electrobiochemical ability to produce energy, which can result in a variety of symptoms like pain and dysfunction.

Nerves transmit an electrical signal or action potential, a signal which travels along the nerve and is controlled by gated channels that allow for the transfer of ions through a cell wall. This requires energy or adenosine triphosphate (ATP); when your ATP (see Chapter N – Nutrients) is low, you find you will crave carbohydrates or sugary foods.

The great news is these signals can be restored and repaired. Unblocking this energy can help promote healing and wellness.

Energy therapies are based upon the appreciation that everything is interconnected through energy fields. Even your emotions and thoughts have energy fields. Everything is made of atoms that produce, emit and receive energy and function at specific frequencies. A healthy human body resonates at a frequency of 62–78 MHz; disease happens when this drops below 58 MHz.

In energy healing, a stimulus is provided which stimulates the nerve cells. Energy in the form of ATP is required to transfer the extracellular molecules to intracellular ones and the energy of the nerve depends on this pump. To simplify this, if you think of the energy stimulus as the voltage, the current is the neural pathway/oscillatory pattern/frequency; the resistance is due to physiological, emotional or environmental factors such as trauma, dehydration, tissue damage, damage to the myelin sheath of the nerve and so on, which creates a weaker current (frequency) and impedes signalling, resulting in slower conduction and a decreased ionic flow. So you need to get the signal back online and retune your body. Restoring this energy promotes healing and wellness.

You may know body energy as chakras which are seven spinning wheels of energy along the spine and are connected to physical, mental and emotional wellness. They are associated with nerves, glands and organs, along with being linked with different abilities, expressions, health and mindful states. When they are in harmony, your energy flows.

Remember that your energy speaks volumes about you and is so much louder than words. You could say it resonates.

You can influence your vibrational frequency or energy in several ways.

Every thought you have emits a frequency out into the universe. This creates resonance and every frequency returns to its source.

Essentially what you think about, you bring about, so every thought you put out there comes back to you. Being mindful and monitoring the quality of your thoughts will help you to cultivate more positive thoughts.

Whom you surround yourself with also directly impacts your energy and frequency. It is important to find those 'radiators' and surround yourself with others who are happy, positive and focussed people. Then you will also enter into this vibration.

Music is really influential. If the tunes are uplifting, happy and joyful, then they influence and elevate your vibrational frequency. So be aware of the words of the music you listen to. The frequency of the music, or rpm, amplitude and volume also directly affect cellular resonance and your own frequency vibration. Along with the emotions that the music evokes, these factors lead you to form attachments with music and makes the resonance even more powerful.

Visual stimulation via the things you see and watch programme the brain. You become more accepting of what you see and it becomes your reality. View things that enhance your mood and help you vibrate at a higher frequency – things that make you feel good.

Being in an organised, clean and uncluttered environment influences your vibrational frequency and your mood, which attracts this into your life and puts into the universe that you are ready to receive more of this. So tidy up. It's amazing how much better you feel after a spring clean.

Think about your verbiage and be mindful of what you say. To keep your frequency high, it is essential to speak positively and take responsibility for your life. Remember that you attract what you put out so start complimenting instead of cursing. Start the day with a positive word and make this a habit. You get to choose what you say. Also, consider what you write … it is called spell-ing for a reason!

Have an attitude of gratitude. Incorporate this into your everyday life. Start by being thankful for one thing; it opens the door for other positive events in your life. You attract exactly what you vibrate into your life.

What frequencies are you putting out into the universe today?

Put out there what you want more of in your life. If you want to be part of the higher vibe tribe, then you need to raise your vibrational frequency – it's quantum physics.

So, consider an abundance of health and happiness, the ability to help others on their journeys, the feeling of sand between your toes, and whatever else brings joy to your life.

> *'If you want to find the secrets of the universe, think in terms of energy, frequency, and vibration.'*
>
> **Nikolai Tesla.**

TOP TIPS

So how can you raise your energy and frequencies so that the problems described in this chapter don't affect you as much?

➤ Where you place your attention is where you place your energy so use this to your benefit.

➤ Start the day with a positive word and make this a habit. You get to choose what you say.

➤ Use affirmations daily or positive statements about you such as, 'I am proud of my achievements.'

➤ Consider how you feel when you are around other people. Surround yourself with 'radiators' and tune in.

➤ Try tapping if you are feeling low energy – gently tapping on the top of your head is like pressing a reset button.

➤ Listen to music that makes your heart sing.

➤ Get out in the sun more often as it recharges your battery.

➤ Get fiery, because when you are living with passion, you are literally 'passing ions' or enhancing your energy.

F − FAILING

This chapter will help you if you:

➢ Want to learn why failure is a good thing

➢ Want to know how to reframe failure

➢ Want top tips on how to deal with failure.

'Failure is an event, not a person.'

Zig Ziglar.

You all try to do your best at everything you undertake. After all, what's the point if you are not doing it well and giving your all? But sometimes things don't go according to 'the plan'.

Sometimes you fail.

When was the first time you failed at something? Take a moment and think back over your life. Often there is a standout moment where you failed at something. It doesn't need to be a spectacular fail, but it should be something you remember. This may stir up some negative or upsetting feelings, but allow yourself to acknowledge these. If you are a classic perfectionist or a type-A personality, this may take a little time.

For me, the first time I ever realised I had failed at anything ever was when I was 18. It left me in a hospital bed and not one of those swanky private numbers. Life was all going well – until it wasn't. I'd failed, badly! Life was turned upside down. This was the first-ever time that something had taken the fire out of me, and I had to start again. Since then, I have failed many times.

Each time you fail at something, it actually helps you. Here's why.

You experience a huge learning curve, develop more ability and listen to what you need. Do you get it right all the time? Absolutely not. And that is okay!

So why am I sharing this? To tell you it's okay to fail! Some of the most successful people you will hear about are huge failures. But you need to tell *yourself* that it's okay to fail.

> *'I've failed over and over again in life, and that is why I succeed.'*
>
> **Michael Jordan.**

Things happen. Through the reframing of it all – to see the positive in the negative – helps you use these events as learning experiences and helps you to grow! You need to tell yourself that it is okay to mess up. It is okay not to be perfect. Fail often, fail hard and know that it all happens for a reason! But see the failures as learning opportunities and treat them as lessons to grow and progress. It's okay if it all turns to sh*t and you fail.

Something else you need to consider is that the biggest difference between successful and unsuccessful people is how they respond to failure. You will face setbacks in life, but you can choose how you respond to them. It sounds cliché, but oftentimes the only things you are in control of are your reactions. When you are faced with an adverse event, yes, you can throw yourself a 'pity party'… but put a time limit on it. Allow yourself to wallow, to be p*ssd, to get angry, whatever, and then shelve it, reflect and review it.

There are lots of people that recommend a little pity party, including me, but the great Zig Ziglar said it best … *'The problem with pity parties is very few people come, and those who do, don't bring presents.'*

When you fail at something, usually one of two things will happen: (1) You think *f*ck it* and give up, or (2) you think *I'll try harder tomorrow*. Neither of these things is wrong and they are valid responses. It doesn't mean you are a failure of a person.

If you think *f*ck it*, you need to consider whether what you have set out to do is achievable and realistic. By this I mean is it within your capabilities? If it is, then simply map out plan B. If it's not, then look at whether you need to achieve it. If so, then what can you do to break it down to make it achievable? You shouldn't be disheartened by this; remember that it's okay to fail. But what you need to do is reassess the goal. If it is currently unattainable, think of smaller steps; how can you break this down into more achievable steps? If you set 'mini goals' which lead up to this larger goal, you are more likely to achieve it! And guess what? Those mini-wins when you achieve your goals are creating consistency in your behaviours. These behaviours become habits. And guess what else – you then have a chance! Whoa, epic!

If you thought, on the other hand, *don't worry, I'll try harder tomorrow* – what if tomorrow never comes? If everything is mañana mañana, are you in fact just putting off starting? If you don't start, how will you know what you can achieve? If you don't start, nothing will change and guess what? You'll be in this same position next year. So stop delaying.

If you missed out on a training session, do something else that's active. If you ate poorly, prepare your next day's meals in advance so there are no excuses. Where there is a will there is a way. Don't be hard on yourself; just take action! Everyone was a beginner once, so never say you can't. Just do the thing because if it is important to you, it's worth making the time for.

Here's a news flash: every one of you is a failure! So, resolve to change that in the next 60 seconds. Be optimistic, be curious, alter your outlook, change your attitude and see everything as an opportunity.

'I have no special talent, I am only passionately curious.'

Albert Einstein.

Failure could be the best thing that could happen because it makes you think about what you want. Is it something you want or something you *think* you should want? Learn to love the process and consider that, even if you fail, you can always catch up or even surpass your expectations.

Looking at this with an altered perspective helps with your clarity around failure and failing. They are essentially two different things and two different mindsets.

Failing is about the process. If you fail at something, this helps you learn from experience by providing you with feedback on what to improve. Failing helps you to develop, enhances your personal growth and creates future progression opportunities.

Failure is when you have given up, sometimes because you've talked yourself out of something before you have even started and sometimes because you are scared of failing, or of succeeding. This is where you have essentially accepted defeat, which doesn't aid your development or your learning and creates no future opportunities for you.

Sometimes life can be a bit 'real' and you can feel like you are in an overwhelming spiral of doom, so simple stuff is what's needed. You need to be there for yourself. After you've thrown your pity party for a day, then just stop. Get outside yourself and do something fun just for the sake of it – something that brings you joy. It can be putting on your favourite tunes and dancing in the house, or perhaps cancelling your appointments and meeting up with friends. Sometimes you just need to remember that life is fun, and even when it feels like sh*t, there is still fun to be made.

> *'It is our choices that show what we truly are,*
> *far more than our abilities.'*
>
> **J. K. Rowling.**

TOP TIPS

When it comes to failure, I have three things I do that I have developed over the past 20 odd years. When I do them, it really helps with my failures.

➢ Have my 'pity party' for one. I set myself a time limit, say an hour. I'll go for a walk or put on some music and dance around the house. No one else is invited.

➢ I look at what failed. I ask questions of myself like was it planned well enough? Did I do everything I could have done? What stood in my way of achieving? What needs changing? I may even discuss it with someone I trust.

➢ If I don't feel it's right for me, then it goes into the f*ck it bucket. I may revisit at a later date, but it means it's not for now. If I feel it is workable, then I unpick things and identify smaller steps to achieve that are wins on the way to achieving what I want.

G – GROUNDING

This chapter will help you if you:

➤ Want to learn what grounding is

➤ Want to know what the effects of grounding are

➤ Want top tips on how to ground yourself.

'Live in the sunshine, swim the sea, drink the wild air.'

Ralph Waldo Emerson.

You are a living, bioelectrical being existing on an electrical planet. All of your cells transmit frequencies (see Chapter E – Energy) or messages that control what happens in your body. So your body operates with bioelectrical communications between cells via charged ionic currents of elements like potassium, calcium and sodium.

Grounding is also known as earthing and is the practice of drawing on the subtle, natural electrical charge that the earth contains to recharge and renew your energy, a bit like recharging a battery. Think about electrical health and safety – everything is 'earthed' or 'grounded' for stability and safety allowing excess electric charge to disperse, as the earth can accept and provide large numbers of electrons.

You contain bioelectricity, as does the earth, in the form of the Schumann resonance. The earth beneath your feet provides a unique energy that directly influences your body. The surface is electrically conductive and contains an unlimited supply of electrons (negatively charged). Grounding is the transfer of electrons from the earth to the body, a process in which the earth balances the body's bioelectric cellular charge. This helps the body to create homeostasis in its internal bioelectrical environment as the negatively charged electrons absorbed from the earth promote the normal functioning of all your body systems. Nobel prize winner Richard Feynman (1965) claimed grounding stabilised the electric potential between the body and the earth.

Everything operates on a frequency, including your cells and body systems. You have multiple frequencies inside you that control your body. The earth is a source of free electrons which also acts as a source of natural antioxidants (see Chapter A – Antioxidants). By donating these electrons to the body, the earth can neutralise and stabilise free radicals that proliferate and cause oxidative stress, inflammation and dysfunction, allowing instead for restoration to happen. It is energy and it is everywhere!

You need to be grounded. A grounded body is healthier and more balanced. It helps you to feel centred, strong, relaxed, solid, less tense, less stressed and stable.

Being in contact with the earth and grounding has numerous benefits and acts as a simple yet extremely effective natural solution to promote optimal wellness. It helps to reduce the body's voltage induced by electromagnetic frequencies (EMFs) in the environment, which in turn reduces inflammation and enhances healing. Remember, though, that grounding is not a 'cure'; it works to normalise your body's natural electrical balance.

Benefits of grounding include: helping to decrease pain and inflammation, reducing free radicals and oxidative stress, reducing stress levels, improving circulation, improving sleep, enhancing mood, and renewing energy and bioelectrical processes supporting nerve conduction.

Earthing enhances parasympathetic nervous system (PNS) activation and vagus nerve signalling, which helps to promote calm, reduces stress, supports the regulation of inflammation, reduces bloating, supports digestion and regulates hormonal rhythms by normalising circadian rhythms.

With the normalising effect upon the parasympathetic branch of the autonomic nervous system, you will notice improved heart rate variability (HRV), the space between heartbeats. A higher HRV is an indication of better recovery and wellness.

A higher HRV, in turn, reduces blood viscosity, which improves circulation and blood oxygen and lowers blood pressure. This leads to improved oxygen and nutrient delivery and waste removal, which supports peripheral circulation, enhanced healing of tissues and nourishment. Having better blood flow supports lymphatic circulation and digestion.

If you feel any of the following, it may be time to get grounded:

➤ Do you become easily distracted, feel like your brain is in a fog, overthink everything, feel anxious or need drama in your life?

➤ Do you need material things to feel happy, obsess about how you look and how others view you?

➤ Do you have inflammation, disturbed sleep, poor circulation, chronic pain or fatigue?

Don't worry, help is at hand and grounding is free and simple to perform.

How does grounding feel?

Well, you may not actually 'feel' anything in particular, though some people notice an overall sense of calm followed by other more physical presentations. You will generally feel more at peace with your authentic self. You may be consciously or subconsciously aware of the sensation.

Some may describe the feeling as floating on clouds, feeling free, being present. Don't worry about how it should feel, just know that it works and just let it be.

For you to know how it feels, you should experience it – just get out on the grass barefoot. However, to try and describe the feeling, if you can, visualise a time when you've been on a beach in the middle of summer on a beautiful day. Think of the moment your toes feel the sand between them; no matter which beach you are on, who you are with or the weather around you, you will feel centred. Feeling that sand beneath your feet does something to your soul – it grounds you and connects you to the earth.

Whenever you're feeling a little off-kilter, ground yourself. Once your feet touch the ground, your body begins to normalise. For you to be grounded, all you need is to be barefoot and in touch with the ground. Shoes act as a barrier to the earth's energy, so you are disconnected. Try it. Get outside and walk barefoot; grassy areas or a beach are ideal locations, or even gardening with your hands in the soil. Be mindful of the sensations and how it feels.

Some other approaches are laying on the ground to connect to the earth, or wild swimming in the sea or lakes.

On the days where the weather is not as favourable, you can still ground outdoors; though, for those of you who are not fond of snow, cold, mud and rain, there are options like grounding footwear or grounding mats.

Like anything, consistency is a must. The more often you ground yourself, the more centred you will feel. It is great to do it first thing in the morning when the sun rises and you drink your morning water as it sets you up well for the day ahead. Stay mindful and present as you are grounding and be aware of your surroundings; keep your eyes open, listen, smell, taste and allow the environment to envelop your senses.

You can try using the 5, 4, 3, 2, 1 approach, which helps you to become more mindful of your surroundings and to utilise your senses. So take a look around and notice 5 things you can see, like the light, the grass, the trees and the people. Then notice 4 things you can feel, like a light breeze, the sun, the rain or the cold. Then notice 3 things you can hear, such as words, the wind in the trees or traffic. Then notice 2 things you can smell, like freshly cut grass or brewed coffee. Finally, notice 1 thing you can taste, like sea air.

Go on – kick off your shoes and let your feet go naked!

TOP TIPS

➤ Take off your shoes and socks and get outside. Stand on the earth – grass, stone, sand or dirt.

➤ Focus your awareness on the bottom of your feet, paying attention to any sensations for at least one minute.

➤ Go for a walk but stay present. Be aware of your environment – the sounds, smells and sensations. If you can do it barefoot, awesome!

➤ Lay on the floor and roll. Yes, I said roll, however you like – give it a go!

➤ Turn off your tech. This will help you to disconnect and then reconnect with your natural energy. Don't believe me? Turn off all of your tech by 9 pm, and let me know how you sleep!

H – HORMONES

This chapter will help you if you:

> Want to know what hormones are

> Want to know how hormones are produced and how they affect you

> Want top tips on how to support your hormonal health.

Hormones are mentioned a lot when it comes to many of your symptoms – especially if you're a woman. 'It's your hormones' is a typical statement. Hormones are a vast subject that comes up consistently. There is in fact a whole branch of study dedicated to hormones called endocrinology, which is an area I have invested my time heavily into as it is a subject close to my own heart.

There's too much to include everything here but the basics and the most common points will be covered.

Hormones are essentially chemical messengers in your body that communicate between your cells, tissues and organs. They can either act locally where they are produced or further away, travelling through the bloodstream to their receptor sites. Hormones are produced in your endocrine glands including the ovaries, testes, pituitary, thyroid, pancreas and adrenals, which often signal each other in sequence and have a cascade effect. Hormones impact your whole body from your metabolism, growth and development, cell function, sexual function, reproduction, sleep and mood among other things.

To put your endocrine system and hormones in context, it's important to know that the entire endocrine system is regulated by minerals, which need to be finely balanced for optimal function. In isolation and in combination, the endocrine organs modulate many systems and processes in the body. So nutrients are super important to your overall wellness and should not be overlooked.

For example, the hypothalamus is in the brain and is the control centre for the endocrine system aiming to maintain homeostasis (balance) in the body and requires chromium for good health. Hormones, such as growth hormone releasing hormone (GHRH), are released, which stimulates the pituitary gland to produce and release growth hormone (GH) into the bloodstream, which affects metabolism and growth.

The pituitary gland, also in the brain, acts as the 'master gland' due to its control over hormones that govern other endocrine glands. It requires adequate manganese for optimal health. It is responsible for secreting oxytocin (helps with bonding), prolactin (encourages post-partum milk production), luteinising hormone (stimulates ovulation and testosterone production), anti-diuretic hormone (signals kidneys to conserve water) and growth hormone (encourages growth and healing).

The pineal gland produces melatonin (see Chapter C – Circadian rhythms) and relies upon iodine and boron for good health.

The thyroid requires iodine and tyrosine to support both the regulation of metabolism and production of thyroxine (T4), which is converted to triiodothyronine (T3) with the help of selenium and calcitonin, which is responsible for the absorption of calcium into bone.

The parathyroid gland supports the distribution of calcium and phosphate.

The thymus supports the immune system by activating your white blood cells' T-cells and T-lymphocytes and requires zinc for optimum function.

The pancreas needs chromium for good function and produces insulin, which is responsible for the conversion of glucose to glycogen and the conversion of excess glucose to fat for storage. The pancreas also produces glucagon, responsible for the conversion of glycogen to glucose for use as energy.

The adrenal glands are reliant upon copper. They produce adrenaline which prepares the body for fight or flight (see Chapter B – Breathing), noradrenaline and cortisol.

The ovaries require selenium for good health and to produce oestrogen (breaks down the uterus wall) and progesterone (supports uterus wall in pregnancy).

The testes also rely on selenium for health and testosterone production.

You may already be most familiar with the 'stress hormone' cortisol, along with the sex hormones from the ovaries called oestrogen and progesterone, and from the testes, testosterone. These hormones are the ones routinely measured in lab tests. They are important to note as they can have a profound effect on your wellness, so we will look into these in a little more detail.

Firstly, it is wise to know a little about how these hormones are produced to know how they affect you. These hormones – cortisol, oestrogen, progesterone and testosterone – are manufactured from a precursor called pregnenolone. Each of these has a vital role in regulating various bodily functions; without this balance, there are compromises in your wellness.

For instance, cortisol, the 'stress hormone', produced in the adrenal glands, allows for fight or flight syndrome – if you need to get away from a tiger, this kicks in. Because we never know when that figurative or literal tiger will appear, cortisol production is always ready, but at the expense of other hormones. When we are highly stressed and enter fight or flight mode, due to the increased cortisol demand, pregnenolone is diverted into the production of cortisol, and the production of hormones like testosterone, oestrogen and progesterone decreases. This is known as the pregnenolone steal – it 'steals' pregnenolone away from other hormone pathways.

Cortisol is not the only hormone produced by the adrenal glands. They also produce aldosterone, which regulates your sodium/potassium levels and, thus, your heart rhythm and blood pressure. Aldosterone signals the kidneys and gut to increase the level of sodium in the blood or the amount of potassium excreted as urine, which stabilises blood pressure. Fluctuations in your heart rhythm are an indication that aldosterone levels are not optimal.

Pregnenolone is made from cholesterol, which is made from low-density lipoproteins (LDL) and needs T3 (from the thyroid) and vitamin A (retinal from meat products) to complete production. So anytime you are stressed or injured, cholesterol production is increased to make a lifesaving hormone – cortisol. The body will always prioritise survival over hormone production. When everything is working well, you will be manufacturing enough pregnanolone from LDL cholesterol to support the appropriate production of testosterone, progesterone, oestrogen and cortisol.

Cholesterol has been labelled 'bad' for a long while; however, it is in every cell of the body and dietary consumption of cholesterol has little to do with your body's production of it. High levels of cholesterol indicate a high oxidative stress level (see Chapter A – Antioxidants) and blocking cholesterol actually increases stress on the body systems. You need to remember that LDL levels will naturally rise to protect your cells, and – to make more cholesterol in response to stress and to produce more cortisol and other hormones – we can sometimes get stuck in this stress cycle.

If you are experiencing symptoms that may be linked to hormones, then testing is a good idea. Cholesterol is a good marker to indicate how well the body is producing hormones.

It is interesting to note that when your cells are under oxidative stress, this lowers your stores of ATP and magnesium and the cell responds by increasing cholesterol production.

If your cholesterol levels aren't optimal, you may experience the manifestation of lots of symptoms like:

➤ memory issues

➤ loss of libido

➤ unexplained muscular pain

➤ blood sugar issues

➤ liver issues

➤ altered mood states (like low mood or worry).

Chronic stress literally impacts you at a cellular level, which affects all your body systems – everything is connected. Your endocrine system works in multiple areas of the body and, depending on the information it receives, dictates what hormones in what quantities are released. So stress can screw with your hormone levels and affect everything from your mood to your weight. Once the hormones get screwed up, it's often a perpetual cycle of symptoms, sub-optimal health care and reduced wellness.

If you are struggling with weight issues, these can be related to the effects of stress and the resultant impact upon your hormones.

If your thyroid is under pressure, then due to the influence on your metabolism, this can lead to weight gain all around. If you have prolonged stress, cortisol acts as a self-preservation mechanism and stores fat around your visceral organs. This can lead to excess weight around the midsection. If you have an issue with the ovaries, then the weight is stored around the hips and lower abdomen. If you have liver issues, then weight tends to be carried around the torso, though the lower limbs are slim.

For women, at certain times of the month, your hormones fluctuate, which has a direct impact on your weight and body composition through to your energy levels and temperature.

A regular cycle contains the following:

> menstruation (days 1–5)
> follicular phase (days 6–14)
> ovulation phase (days 13–15)
> luteal phase (days 15–28).

Your period is the perfect time to slow down and relax as energy levels are lowest. So take some time out.

During the follicular phase, you have an increased tolerance to pain and can tolerate more physically and mentally. You will thermoregulate better, have less fatigue, increased strength and better recovery from the activity you undertake. Your basal metabolic rate (BMR) and energy expenditure will decrease, so you will also have extra energy available.

Towards the end of the follicular phase, testosterone (supports building and growth) and oestrogen (protects muscle from being broken down) are at their highest and you can probably tolerate the most intense levels of activity around here. So, if you are training for an event, then here is where you can increase the intensity.

During the luteal phase and post-ovulation, your core body temperature increases and you may find it difficult to modulate your temperature. This is caused by fluctuations in progesterone. You may feel hot, fatigued, dehydrated and a little uncoordinated. Your BMR increases and you are probably craving sweet foods as your progesterone peaks. Try not to demolish the whole packet of biscuits, though. Lower intensity of activity is called for here, like maybe just a walk.

During perimenopause, your ovaries stop producing their previous levels of hormones. This means that you have lower levels of oestrogen and progesterone and, when oestrogen drops, you get hot flashes. Your adrenal glands then become your main producer of oestrogen via cholesterol. We know when you are stressed you are asking your adrenal glands to produce cortisol and other stress hormones. So you won't be making as much oestrogen, which can lead to hot flashes. For men, testosterone level drops as you age. This can lead to increased abdominal fat, lowered libido, decreased muscle mass and aggressiveness.

Lifestyle and environment affect your hormones more than anything else and are mostly modifiable (see Chapter L – Lifestyle).

So how are your hormones?

If you want 'healthy hormones', there are some simple things you can do to support your wellness. Making little changes over time makes a huge difference, though you may require additional advice and support from a holistic health professional.

TOP TIPS

➢ Remove or circumnavigate any stressors, or work on better coping strategies. If you are highly stressed, then things like meditation, grounding, removing technology and movement may all help.

➢ You can get your hormone levels tested. This gives a snapshot of what is happening and acts as a useful guide but is not really definitive. The salivary test for cortisol and the DUTCH test for hormones are currently the best out there (see references).

➢ The best thing to do is influence your immediate environment to reduce the internal and external stressors. Blue light blocking glasses, red light and reducing artificial light exposure especially at night are key.

1 – INTENTIONS

This chapter will help you if you:

➤ Want to know what intentions are

➤ Want to know why you should use them

➤ Want top tips on how to implement intentions in your life.

'All that counts in life is intention.'

Andrea Bocelli.

Setting goals, targets and intentions is something you usually associate with January and New Year's resolutions, when you start thinking about change and the whole new year – and a new you.

However, you don't have to wait until January for a period of reflection, growth and change. Oftentimes setting your intentions may be the better route to take than waiting to make a resolution.

Have you ever resolved to change something for a new you?

There is nothing wrong with wanting to make a change. Resolutions, though, often place lots of pressure on you, especially if it's something big or really important to you.

You know how it feels to have 'fallen off the wagon' – you skip a gym session, you eat a packet of hobnobs, you don't complete the online course you signed up for, you sprain an ankle and can't do your daily runs? Feels pretty crappy, right?

A resolution is something that can often make you feel like you haven't achieved what you set out to do – like you have actually failed. It can be pretty discouraging and disheartening. There's that crappy feeling again.

An alternative option is to place intentions. Intentions are communicating what you set out to do, though with a looser structure than a SMART (specific, measurable, achievable, realistic and time-framed) goal. Put your intentions out there in public, write them down, tell people, put them into the universe and feel all the feelings related to this and what it would be like to already have or be doing them.

When you have intentions, you are a little kinder to yourself. If you miss a gym session, it's okay, you just pick up where you left off. It's not the end of the world. You still have the same motivation, the same focus, but if you mess up, you simply start again. It sounds so much better and let's face it – life happens when you are busy making plans, so you have to adjust and adapt!

Having things to aim for is a fantastic motivator but being fluid in your thinking is key as nothing is set in concrete. This is a good thing because if something doesn't go your way, you often feel disappointed; but, once you realise that, it may simply be a change of intention that is needed and a switch of your focus. Then the level of stress in your life will dramatically reduce.

How many times have you thought, *if I could just do/have/be this one thing, my life will be so much better*? Think back. Was it better when you got there? More often than not, it hasn't made a difference to better your life, or you have already moved on to the next thing and not celebrated your achievement.

Have you ever worked at something for an extended period of time, only to realise that once you achieve it, it's not what you want? Have you spent time, effort and energy striving away to reach a target only to see that, once you get there, the goalposts have moved – that achieving something you longed for doesn't change the way you feel, so you are left, at best, reassessing, reevaluating and rewriting your targets and, at worst, feeling bereft and adrift?

If you don't achieve what you set out to do, it's okay; if you do achieve it, and it isn't all it was cracked up to be, it's also okay. You are not the same person as you were yesterday and you are different from the person that you will become. Some of the intentions that you may set yourself are long term and a great deal can happen along the way to fulfilling them. They may change, you may fulfil them earlier than you expect, or you may have set the bar too high; you may become unable to achieve them. So what? Intentions can change too!

Remember that your intentions are adaptable and there is wiggle room and flexibility. In many instances, the process is just as important as the end target. So long as you're trying your best, who could ask for more?

Reflect. Reassess. Reevaluate. Rewrite your intentions as needed. Make this a habit by returning to these every month to help refocus you.

'Our intention creates our reality.'

Wayne Dyer.

You should have an idea of what you intend to achieve. It doesn't necessarily need to be a formalised plan, but without clear intentions, you just tend to drift along. In some cases, there is nothing wrong with this at all. But if you have an intention and are aiming to fulfil this without having considered some of the actions needed to get you there, then you probably won't achieve it.

It doesn't need to be a minute-by-minute gameplay, unless that's your thing; but for most of you, even the best-laid plans can't account for every eventuality in life. If you have something in mind, it is worth considering some of the smaller hurdles you may need to cross to achieve this. For example, if you are aiming to be a world champ, then you probably need to qualify through opens and regionals. So are you just going to turn up at these races or events? Or are you going to consider what you need to do to perform at your best? Are you going to set your intentions and take action?

Intentions can be something that are best talked through with a coach or mentor. Most of us don't like to be dictated to, but having a little help in mapping out what's required to get you there may help and you may achieve smaller wins along the way.

However, if, like me, you're not aiming for world domination – just to be a better version of yourself – then you want to set yourself achievable benchmarks on the way to your overall aim.

Simply putting your intentions out there, making them known, having them in your thoughts and ensuring they are written down or placed visually on your dream board is important to keep them in the forefront of your mind if you are to accomplish things.

In any instance, go slow and steady, bit by bit, step by step and start an intentional plan!

TOP TIPS

Here are some recommendations to help you implement positive intentions, love the process and journey, and not just get to the end result.

➤ Have something to aim for or something you'd like to accomplish and break this down into at least three actionable steps.

➤ Be kind to yourself. If life happens, don't beat yourself up. Quit the negative self-talk. Just pick up where you left off and continue with your intentions.

➤ Remember you are awesome and your cells resonate with the frequency you emit (see Chapter E – Energy). Tell yourself a positive story, and – even if you don't get to your intended end result – you may have, in fact, achieved something better along the way.

J – JOURNALLING

This chapter will help you if you:

➤ Want to know what journalling is

➤ Want to know how journalling can support your self-care

➤ Want top tips on how to get the most from journaling.

'Fill your paper with the breathings of your heart.'
William Wordsworth.

The first thing to do is to buy a beautiful notebook and a beautiful pen. If you love stationery as much as I do, then this is a great place to start.

Journalling allows you to get the thoughts, feelings and events that are happening in your life out of your head and onto paper, which helps reduce feelings of overwhelm and creates what I like to call 'brain space'. This means you can go back to things later and review them with a clearer perspective. Writing things down can also help if you are struggling with overthinking and procrastination.

So how can you begin your journalling?

'Brain dumping'. This is where you put anything that's in your head down on the paper. Anything. Just write. There doesn't need to be any order to it. It doesn't need to be in any particular style. Just get it out of your head. Doing this on a late Sunday afternoon once the weekend is almost over, after you've had time to ponder, helps refresh your system for the start of the week on a Monday.

You can use your journal to support your self-care by helping you to focus upon your priorities, reducing chaos and overwhelm. The thing is, once something is out of your head, this allows you space to think and with more clarity as the thoughts are no longer swirling around in your head but are now there on the page. You can go back to them and then pick out one thing that you want to work on. Only pick one as you will only focus fully on one thing at a time. Then you can work on this.

Your journal can be used to nourish your body, mind and soul by adding your intentions, completing your actions and creatively pondering your reflections to enhance your organisation, productivity and achievement.

Another recommendation with journalling is to write down what you are grateful for. Starting to commit your gratitude to paper in your journal will help you to stay present. Making it a daily practice in which you remind yourself to be grateful allows you to become more in touch with your true self by having a positive impact upon your emotions, renewing your energy and restoring your wellbeing. When you feel better and more like yourself, you find you are more helpful, generous and compassionate, which actively supports your wellness journey. When you read your gratitude list back, you'll realise that you have lots of good already there.

Your thoughts influence your being. Being present and aware of your thoughts will take time and practice; however, you will also notice how much those negative thinking patterns impact your life. The benefits of practising gratitude thus include: supporting your immune system, improved tolerance to aches and pains, a brighter outlook, lower blood pressure and improved sleep quality that leaves you feeling more refreshed when you wake.

When you start, it is what I call a 'gratitude adjustment' – being grateful for life and for the things life gives you means the more life there is to be grateful for. Sometimes it is a small shift in perspective that may bring gratitude, fulfilment and an abundance of happiness into life.

'Journal writing is a voyage to the interior.'

Christina Baldwin.

Starting a gratitude journal and writing down everything you are grateful for daily will help you stay present and aware.

Gratitude positively affects your vibrational frequency. This is a practice that you should incorporate into your life now because the frequency you emit attracts like frequencies so it boosts your cellular resonance (see Chapter E – Energy).

You can always be a little more grateful. It's easy to sit there and think about the things you don't have and what you lack in life. This is actually the way your brain is programmed – with a negative bias. But you can work on it. You can make the choice.

Like anything, if you practise, you get better. With the recent advances in neuroplasticity research, we know you can change the way your brain functions. Your neurons can change. Physiologically, it is the neurons that fire together that wire together and, in effect, become more synchronous and effective. So, if you practise something that becomes habitual, it stands to reason that you can change the way you think at a cellular level and your patterning changes.

You can use this as a kickstart on your wellness journey. Trust me, it works.

Be grateful for everything – for the good things and what you consider to be bad. Be grateful for all your experiences and the lessons you have learned. Gratitude opens the door for more good things to happen positively in your life. If you are experiencing tougher times, try to pick out one thing, one positive thing, from the day, and be grateful for this. No matter how small it may seem, it is helping you on your path to wellness.

All you need to do is commit daily to stating one thing you are grateful for. Be specific as to why you're grateful, how it makes you feel and when it occurs. This detail is the key to nailing those actions and sustainable changes.

To promote gratitude, remember the hard times you once experienced. When you remember how difficult life has been in the past and how far you have come, you set the platform for gratefulness.

TOP TIPS

➤ Each week, take a time-out and 'brain dump' things onto paper. Get things out of your head and into your journal.

➤ Take a moment during your day to be grateful for something. It could be your body, your mind, your gifts, your talents or the people, places and events you experience or things you enjoy. Doing so gives you the potential to interweave a sustainable practice of gratefulness into your day. Write these into your journal.

➤ Feel the feels! You need to feel how it is to be grateful. This is the key to change.

K – KINDNESS

This chapter will help you if you:

➤ Want to know what kindness is

➤ Want to know the effects of kindness

➤ Want top tips on how to be kinder.

There is always lots of talk about being kind, so let's take a deeper look. Kindness can be described as a personal quality where you demonstrate friendliness, generosity or consideration of others for no personal gain. It is easy to do, costs mostly nothing and can mean the world. Let's face it, there are lots of simple things you can do to be kind.

Why not look at what makes you happy and how you can help and support others? There is even a 'World Kindness Day' on the 13th of November each year. However, it shouldn't be limited to just one day. Kindness should be a daily practice.

One of my favourite quotes is '*Kindness is love with its work boots on*' (The House Bunny). You could express this as kindness being love in action. It can rejuvenate and refresh you and provide strength and compassion.

Whether you choose to offer kindness with small acts or big gestures, kindness is where you are expressing care, concern or compassion for others in the world – often when they expect it least and need it most.

Kindness is a choice.

First and foremost – be kind to yourself.

The best advice is always to care for yourself first. You can't do your best if you are under par, and you also need to practise kindness while having clear boundaries. If you don't put your parameters in place, you may find that people begin to take more than you have to offer. This is detrimental to you and your wellness. So remember this simple mantra of 'do no harm, take no sh*t'. If something begins to take more of a toll on you, then you need to stop and reassess.

It's super important to be kind to yourself and to those around you as kindness is contagious. People learn from seeing others in action. If they see you and your kindness, they are likely to emulate this, especially children – they see and copy everything! Can you remember what it's like when you offer simple acts of kindness, like smiling at a stranger, saying thank you or holding a door for the next person? Feels good, right? These are all acts of kindness that are simple, and by offering them to others, they are likely to reciprocate or repeat the act. This positive reinforcement will remind you to practise kindness.

To improve at something, you have to practise it. Kindness is no different. To make this a part of your world, you need to show it and practise it daily. If you are intentional about practising kindness, it becomes a habit or a behavioural pattern and soon, automatic.

By being kind to others, you are also being kind to yourself. It's a win-win. When you complete an act of kindness, it elicits an emotion such as love, compassion or joy. You release several hormones including dopamine, oxytocin, serotonin, endorphins and growth hormone, which are associated with satisfaction, pleasure, feeling good, elevated wellness and restoration respectively. The more often you do it, the more the prolonged sense of improved wellbeing.

One way to demonstrate kindness is by paying it forward. It's also the easiest way to benefit someone else, and yourself. It simply means doing something for another person, with no expectation of recognition or anything in return. And it's contagious. Whether it be for the feel-good factor you get or seeing the joy on another's face, the likelihood is that the recipient will then 'pay it forward' and pass the love on to someone else by performing their own act of kindness.

So, when someone does something for you, instead of paying that person back directly, you pass it on to another person instead. Paying it forward can be a random act of kindness or it can be to someone you know is in need. If you're unsure, maybe ask the person what you could do for them. Where I live, there is a Facebook group where people are kind to each other and pay it forwards regularly.

By being kind to someone else, not only will it possibly make their day, but soulful revenue is always returned to the benefactor through selfless acts. Kindness will come back to you. If you put kindness out there, it will be returned; it's the karmic law of the universe. Even if it's just a smile, a compliment of 'love the dress' to a stranger, it will make you feel good and you are paying it forward. The person you address is also likely to perpetuate the cycle!

It doesn't need to be a grandiose gesture; rather, it's often the smallest acts of kindness that truly mean the most.

'Sometimes it takes only one act of kindness and caring to change a person.'

Jackie Chan.

At the end of each day, you may want to reflect and ask yourself where your focus is, how you treated others and whether you acted with kindness. This is a great way to self-improve and be more mindful of your impact on the world.

The world can always do with more kindness and by making the conscious choice to be kind, you could change someone else's world. So smile at the people you meet, hold doors open for them in stores, hug your family and let others know you appreciate them.

When you are considering kindness, you can also review the specific words, actions or intentions that come to mind. Considering the impact you have makes these acts more personal and meaningful to you and you are more likely to incorporate these actions daily so they do indeed become habits. Emotions and feelings have a huge part in your habits, so consider when you were last kind. How did this make you feel? When someone was last kind to you, how did this make you feel? By identifying these feelings – and they likely were positive, joyful, happy and loving feelings – you know you can replicate these by continuing to be kind.

Performing random acts of kindness is a lovely thing to do and it is more common than you may think.

If you'd like to give it a try, then here are some gentle reminders of actions that you could take:

➢ Smile at someone.

➢ Compliment someone, like 'I love your dress, it really suits you.'

➢ When you're paying for your coffee in the local coffee shop, why not pay for a cuppa for the next person in line too.

- ➤ When you're out and about, why not go and chat with a homeless person and ask if there is something you may be able to do for them.

- ➤ When you're next shopping, buy a little extra and donate it to a food bank.

- ➤ Go and chat to your neighbour and ask if there is anything they need help with, like gardening, shopping, dog walking or whatever you can think of.

- ➤ Look at local online groups and see what people are asking for.

- ➤ Pay someone's bill at the checkout.

- ➤ Leave a big tip for a stressed-out server.

- ➤ Donate unwanted items to a charity shop.

- ➤ Help to carry someone's bags.

- ➤ Buy someone a sandwich.

- ➤ Volunteer your time.

- ➤ Give a warm hug.

- ➤ Hold the door for someone.

- ➤ Say thank you.

- ➤ Tell someone you appreciate them.

- ➤ Help someone with a problem.

- ➤ Share heartfelt words.

- ➤ Be present and notice when someone needs support.

- ➤ Anything else you can think of for which you stand to receive no financial gain or expect public thanks.

Whatever it is you decide to do, be kind.

'A smile is a curve that sets everything straight.'

Phyllis Diller.

Don't be surprised if some heart-based actions or surprises come your way because, when you are swept up by soulful generosity that comes from the heart, you are sending out a message to the universe and attracting more of this back to you. It is contagious energy.

If you are the recipient and it gives you that 'feel-good' factor and fills you up, then pass the baton along and give some kindness to someone else. Look for the magic showing up in your life, that stuff that makes you go, 'Wow, that's amazing.' Hold onto that feeling. Then pass it along.

If you have the chance to make someone happy – just do it. Sometimes people may be struggling silently; maybe your act of kindness could make their day.

Don't ever get tired of being a good person, with a good heart. People like you are what give the world hope.

So, I want to offer kindness and pay it forward as well.

Maybe no one has told you how amazing you are … 'You are amazing.'

Maybe no one has said thank you today … 'Thank you for all that you do.'

Maybe no one has congratulated you for all that you do … 'What you are doing is awesome; thank you for bringing light into the world.'

Now go ahead and do it for someone else!

What would happen if you performed one act of kindness a day for the next 30 days?

TOP TIPS

Simple steps to being kinder:

➤ Start simple – begin with a smile at someone else. The likelihood is this will be immediately returned.

➤ Find out what you can do for someone by asking them what they need – and then show them some magic.

➤ Perform a random act of kindness with the knowledge that you have done something lovely for another person.

➤ When you are looking to build actions into your life, do so gradually and not to your own detriment. Set your boundaries and start small.

➤ Ask yourself what energy you wish to convey to the world and how you may do this through kindness.

➤ Try one small act of kindness a day for 30 days and make a note in your journal of how this makes you feel and the responses you received.

L – LIFESTYLE

This chapter will help you if you:

➤ Want to know the importance and effects of lifestyle

➤ Want to know how to identify your own lifestyle habits

➤ Want top tips on how to enhance your lifestyle for improved wellness.

Lifestyle is your individual way of living. This is one of the most impactful factors upon your wellness and one that you have huge choices about.

Your lifestyle includes factors like your activity levels, sleeping patterns, eating habits, hydration levels, social interactions, mental agility and how you deal with stress. The choices that you make and actions that you take daily around these elements and how you choose to live your life has a direct influence upon your wellness and defines not only who you are but how you are.

Optimal lifestyle choices promote wellness, reduce the risk of health conditions and increase your productivity.

If you are looking to improve your wellness, then read on.

Epigenetics is how your genes express themselves relative to your environment, your nutrition, thoughts, behaviours, experiences and emotions. Over time, your genes express their experience and this affects how your genes work. It can be like flicking a switch – sometimes your lifestyle turns genes on and sometimes it turns them off. For example, if you are consistently exposed to toxins in your environment, then your genes will respond and you will manifest symptoms.

The daily practices you have and the actions you perform from things like brushing your teeth to morning coffee to the soap you use and to hugging friends all influence your wellness. These actions become your daily routine, which turn into your habits and behaviours and which ultimately develop the characteristics that make you who you are and form your personality. These things that you practise and train yourself to do become the long-term behaviours you display. The small steps you take daily impact your long-term outcomes.

An ideal lifestyle would have you living an optimal life in optimal wellness. Adopting a lifestyle that nourishes your body, mind and soul for optimal quality of life is ideal. But you can start by simply making better choices.

If you want to make changes to your lifestyle, there are many things you can implement.

Looking to the future can sometimes leave you frozen with indecision over the volume of options and information available. One of the best ways to positively influence your wellness is to reduce your stress, step away from the information highway and disconnect for a while so that you can reconnect with yourself.

You can find lots of information and gain knowledge relatively easily but taking action and implementing it takes more energy.

So take a moment to reflect on your current lifestyle, identify where you can make modifications, set your intentions and then take action.

Reflect on your habits right now and note down the following:

- ➤ What are you doing with your time? Are you spending it making enquiries or doing?
- ➤ Are you scrolling through the online space looking for inspiration, rather than simply doing the thing?
- ➤ Can you identify three beneficial habits you are currently carrying out?
- ➤ Can you identify three non-beneficial habits that you have?

Now that you have reflected, take a moment to note down what your optimal life would look like:

- ➤ Consider what this ideal would include. Think about your daily activity, nutrition, movement, sleep, thoughts and so on.
- ➤ Consider how you spend your free time, downtime, leisure activities, etc.
- ➤ Consider what is needed for all this to become your reality.

Now set out your intentions:

- ➤ Consider what is it that you intend to achieve?
- ➤ Now identify the actions you will need to take. What will you do to achieve this?

By taking the time to consider and note this down, you are essentially writing your life blueprint for your optimal life. It's a powerful activity that helps reduce the overwhelm and motivates you into taking action, which acts as a catalyst for change.

For example, if you need to look at your water intake, by writing it down you take ownership of it and the clarity reminds you that you need to drink more.

Start right now. Implement something today and work it into your daily life because taking action builds momentum.

Bring a goal or intention to mind and write it down. It can be as big as you like as you can then look at making it achievable and realistic by breaking it down into smaller steps or targets. Oftentimes, wanting a whole lifestyle overhaul can be off-putting, so starting with small actions can be beneficial.

By focussing on little stepping stones and having more manageable chunks, you are more likely to be motivated towards the bigger picture every time you achieve one of the smaller wins. The biggest factor that makes the difference is the daily actions you take – the tiny little steps taken on a regular and consistent basis to achieve the bigger goal.

There are 1440 minutes in a day. That's 24 hours. There are 7 days in a week, 28–31 days in a month and 365–366 days in a year. This is the number of opportunities available for you to make actionable, daily steps, consistently over time, to implement changes and maintain sustainable habits.

> *'Every moment is a fresh beginning.'*
>
> **T.S. Eliot.**

You are aiming for 80% compliance to promote your success. If you decide on 2 actions a day over 10 days, this is 20 actions for 100% success; 80% is 16 out of the 20. If you do 3 things every day for 30 days, that's 90 things total and 100% success, which is ideal. Realistically 80% is more achievable. This could be 3 things over 24 days, or 2 things a day for 30 days and 4 days with 3 things a day, which is 72 things total. This is because life happens when you make plans – and sometimes you need to give yourself a break. By aiming for 80%, this is you, still achieving!

Think about this. If you do one thing every day for a year, you will be 365 times more practised at that thing, so you could essentially change your wellness in a year. What one thing could you do today, and repeat every day, for the rest of the year, to help implement a change in your life that will enhance your wellness?

How can you be the best version of yourself today?

Focus on you each day and the things you can implement to live your best life. Believe in living in the present, being in the moment and being the best version of yourself as the one you want to bring to the world.

Don't stress; do your best.

TOP TIPS

- ➤ Choose to make a change to improve your wellness.
- ➤ Reflect on your current lifestyle and identify where you can make changes.
- ➤ Decide what your overall aim is and then break this down into smaller steps. Start with daily action(s) you will take and look to build on this over time.
- ➤ Set your intentions.
- ➤ Take action.
- ➤ Aim for 80% achievement of your chosen action. Sometimes it is a good idea to mark this off on a checklist or in your journal.
- ➤ Reevaluate your intention after 30 days.

M – MOVEMENT

This chapter will help you if you:

➢ Want to know the importance of movement

➢ Want to know how movement affects you

➢ Want top tips on adding movement into your life.

'Movement is life.'

Jules Verne.

Human beings are designed to move. You are not designed to be inanimate and lay or sit around and remain in a lethargic state. The body works best when it is active so it can support the gross motor functions such as walking and lifting as well as the movement of your organs and bodily fluids.

Any movement that you undertake is a form of physical activity, but it doesn't mean that you need to undertake structured exercise for you to be active. Movement constitutes any muscular actions that require energy expenditure – so you probably move more than you realise.

Whether you call it movement, exercise or physical activity, these terms will typically have different associations for you, which are influenced by your history, perceptions and beliefs. Generally, though, a mindset shift is needed to get on board with the view that movement is something your body needs and enjoys.

Often, exercise may be seen as a formalised activity; as such, it can be a chore, something to tick off the to-do list, so you may not complete daily exercise because you feel you don't have the time. Exercise can also bring up images such as working out at the gym, team games, or jogging or spin class, all with the aim of burning calories and 'getting fitter', perhaps as a way to control things or even as a form of punishment if you have 'fallen off the wagon'.

However, movement isn't just about exercising. Movement is far more inclusive and involves being intuitive about what feels good to your body. It's about the ability to connect with how your body feels and listening to what it needs. This helps to nurture a healthy relationship with your body and find ways to ensure that movement is enjoyable for you.

Think about what you enjoy: walking the dog, dancing, going to the park with your children, roller-skating, gardening, stretching, rock pooling, cleaning the house, hiking. Experiment with different things and allow yourself to discover ways you can incorporate movement and activity into your life, without forcing yourself to complete things you know you won't enjoy.

Having a loose structure or plans pencilled into the diary is a great idea. Having a rigid structure, though, might pose too much pressure for some of you, so allow yourself wiggle room and have a list of alternatives that you can incorporate if events don't go as planned. It's about having some kind of balance between connecting with your body and how it feels and mindfully engaging in intentional movement to support your body, mind and soul.

You can perform movement every single day and you don't need to be in your best workout clothes to do it. Movement promotes flow and when your body systems flow, they work in synchronous harmony; your energy flows and you are in alignment.

Changing your mindset will help you to make space for incorporating movement into your daily life without pressure, without expectations of how it should look or how long you should be doing it – and just simply doing it.

Life is not about pushing yourself all the time. You need to give yourself a break when your body calls for it. So paying attention to your body is essential for wellness. It can be good to have some structured exercise in your schedule, especially if you treat it like an appointment you won't miss; but you should always tailor this to your needs and not complete things for the sake of it, or to the detriment of your health and wellbeing.

Daily movement is essential to your wellbeing, though everything should be in balance. Movement promotes the 'feel good' hormones – oxytocin, dopamine, serotonin and endorphins; but, since your body treats all stress in the same way, completing too much and adding to your stress levels is detrimental. So, if you are pushing yourself both physically and mentally to complete an exercise session, especially if you are already under stress, this may create less of a positive benefit and actually add to the stress on your system. If there aren't enough antioxidants to combat the free radicals produced, this creates oxidative stress, inflammation and, in the longer term, can lead to dysfunction (see Chapter A – Antioxidants).

So having a workout programme doesn't mean you are automatically healthy. It is important to consider how you move if you are already stressed. For example, high-intensity exercise on an already stressed-out system can be counterproductive to recovery and healing because the nervous system doesn't differentiate between the source of stress.

However, you can complete restorative, gentle movement to support the down-regulation of the nervous system and promote overall relaxation through, for example, breathwork, tai chi, yoga and gentle stretching.

Your body houses a huge number of awesome structures that work in synchronicity for you to function. If you don't pay attention to what they need, then – much like with your car engine if you don't give it what it requires – you have to bring on the professionals. If you are overexerting yourself, moving incorrectly or too much, perhaps restricting calories or ditching specific food groups, this all increases the stress on the body. So, if you are feeling below par, then your body is not performing optimally.

Perform movement that matches your body's needs by listening to it. Avoid overtraining and rest when necessary.

The body is super smart. It always wants to be in a state of balance. This means it will take shortcuts, cheat or compensate for how you move when those movements are less than optimal to preserve that balance. Whether that's resisting movements or incorporating accessory muscles to support the movement, it is all about protection and prevention of harm. Oftentimes you need to rewrite the instructions and show the body an alternative approach through physical rehabilitation.

For example, your visual system controls many things but did you know that your eyes can facilitate or inhibit your movement?

Try leaning backwards as you look down, then lean backwards as you look up. Which one felt easier? Looking up facilitates extension movements, so leaning backwards should feel easier. Now try moving your eyes to the right and rotating your upper body right. Then try it as you move your eyes left but rotate to the right. Which one felt easier? Moving your eyes to the right as you rotate right facilitates the movement.

So you can work to change movement patterns by integrating the timing of the movement with eye movements. For example, leaning forward and moving the eyes downwards or reaching out to the left and moving the eyes left at the same time helps bring complex patterns into your everyday. As everything is linked together, this makes the movement more complex.

Some of the benefits of daily movement, especially if the movements are complex, include improved cognitive function and memory, enhanced sleep quality, reduced pain sensation, reduced anxiety and low mood, and enhanced functionality of the body.

Most movement influences the brain but complex movements in which you are engaged in the process of learning as you move have further benefits during skill acquisition – think of coordination-dominant activities, like dance and hand–eye coordination tasks.

Complex tasks drive blood flow to the brain and reward complex movement with the release of dopamine and endorphins.

The brain responds to and increases communication with a body engaged in complex movements. So incorporating more complex movements enhances how the brain works, including improved memory, cognition, spatial awareness and attention. Think of crawling patterns, changed body orientation and juggling coordination tasks.

Higher-level skills take a longer time to master so learning is not a linear process.

Daily movement also adds to your NEAT (non-exercise activity thermogenesis) – the energy you expend during your everyday activities, like walking, cleaning and gardening; this is in addition to the calories you use whilst sleeping, eating or undertaking exercise.

Additionally, you need to move for your lymphatic and vascular systems to work efficiently. Muscular movement and diaphragmatic breathing are necessary to move your lymphatic fluid. When you're in pain, the last thing you want to do is move; therefore, the system will become even more stagnated.

So how can you move more?

You are designed to move, so think about all the ways you *can* move.

Here are some ideas for you: walk barefoot, bounce around your living room, dance in the office, shimmy up the stairs, stand whilst on the phone, do a little cleaning every day, use the stairs rather than the lift, park a little further away from the store, go to the park with the kids and join in … whatever. Just move. You are all different, so select the things that bring you joy and add more of them in.

TOP TIPS

Whatever movement means to you, be sure to add it to your day.

➤ Select some simple ways to add movement to your day.

➤ If you tend to get to the end of the day and haven't moved, be sure to schedule time into your day to move.

➤ Think of ways to make the movement in your life essential, and fun! If it's fun, you are more likely to do it.

N – NUTRIENTS

This chapter will help you if you:

➤ Want to know what nutrients you need

➤ Want to know the importance of nutrients in your diet

➤ Want top tips on how to incorporate nutrients into your diet.

'The food you eat can be the safest and most powerful form of medicine or the slowest form of poison.'

Ann Wigmore.

A nutrient is something essential for the maintenance of life, growth, your overall condition and wellness. Your body needs adequate nutrients to support itself and sustain the various bodily processes that contribute to your being well.

You are composed of around 70 trillion cells working to keep you functioning and well. If you nourish your cells, they will flourish. If cells lose their ability to generate energy over long periods, the result can manifest in symptoms and feeling unwell. The ageing process also speeds up as your cells try to renew themselves more often.

Your cells require several nutrients to maintain efficiency and effectiveness. So making choices which support your wellness are significantly important. You need macronutrients in the form of carbohydrates, proteins and fats, and micronutrients in the form of minerals and vitamins. The foodstuffs you eat package the energy transfer of electrons from plants to animals. This process is essential to deliver electrons to the inner mitochondrial membrane of the cells, where you can use the power of the sun's electrons to make chemical energy in adenosine triphosphate (ATP), the body energy currency (see Chapter E – Energy).

However, foods are not as nutrient-dense as they once were due to soil being depleted of nutrients through industrialised farming and the use of chemicals and pesticides. Thus, many of you are actually overfed and undernourished, which means you have too many calories and not enough nutrients to sustain wellness. This can be compounded through many people's inability to optimally digest and absorb nutrients from their food and who therefore don't benefit from the available nourishment in the food. Essentially, this means expensive poop!

What you should look to achieve is consuming whole foods. These are organic, nutrient-dense, unprocessed foods like fruits, vegetables, nuts and seeds, and pastured meats that are rich in nutrients and antioxidants and support the body's systems.

So what should you be eating to support wellness? A little of everything is wise. It's never a one-size-fits-all approach; discernment along with mindful choices is key. The nutritious stuff should take priority and be in the majority as this is supporting the body. Though a little of the indulgent stuff can actually support your immune system since it detoxes and removes the effects of the more processed stuff on the body functions.

VEGETABLES

Try green vegetables that are leafy and cruciferous (like broccoli); steamed or lightly sautéed – either in water, coconut oil or pastured butter – is the better option if you're cooking. Though, honestly, if you can eat two portions of any veg a day, then that's awesome; it's even better if they're organic or homegrown. Yes, these can prove to be expensive, but if you are getting your nutrients from foods, then there is less need to bother with supplementation. Soups made with bone broth to support collagen formation can also be a great option and a great way to get your veggies and nutrients in.

FRUITS

An ideal time to consume these is in the morning, following your water. Where you can, select organic, ripe, local and seasonal options. Consider: apples, apricots, avocados, berries (blueberries, blackberries, raspberries, strawberries), cherries, lemons, limes, oranges, passionfruit, peaches, plums and pomegranates. Another option is juicing with any combinations of fruits along with water or coconut water. Try to avoid pre-made or packaged options as they contain preservatives. Juicing offers readily available nutrients, quick energy and nutrient uptake, less stress on the body and energy requirements for digesting.

CARBOHYDRATES

These are the sugars, starches and fibres found in fruits, grains, vegetables and milk products. Have some with every meal to support restoration and support, metabolism and detoxification.

PROTEINS

These are the meats, fish, eggs and dairy products. Organic pastured meats are the best option; the cheaper cuts, like shin of beef, often have more connective tissue and are thus better for you due to the gelatine content. Organic, free-range poultry is the best option; if you're having a Sunday roast, use the remains to make bone broth that can then be used in your soups. When it comes to fish, sardines are a great choice and, due to their size, very little contamination occurs. Eggs should be organic and free-range and are great for cell nutrition. Dairy is not for everyone but if you can, use raw dairy, or at the least un-homogenised; parmigiano-reggiano, feta and gouda are decent cheese options.

FATS

Avoid refined fats and poor quality oils, which are inflammatory. Grass-fed butter and duck fat in moderation are better options, along with coconut oil for cooking due to its high heat point (more stable).

VITAMINS & MINERALS

An optimal intake of micronutrients supports the body's capacity for repair and restoration. Here are some of the micronutrients you need:

> ➤ B vitamins are involved in metabolic processes in every cell in the body – found in eggs, leafy greens and red meat.

> ➤ Vitamin C is a cofactor in collagen synthesis, so it's essential for regenerating tissues – found in citrus fruits.

> ➤ CoQ10 is present in high quantities in the heart muscle and is essential in the production of ATP or energy – found in fatty fish like sardines.

> ➤ Vitamin E is a fat-soluble antioxidant located in your cell membranes which helps to prevent lipid peroxidation (damage of fats and cellular structures) – found in almonds and pumpkin.

> ➤ Vitamin D, or calcitriol, the bioavailable form, is transported to your organs in the bloodstream, where it regulates calcium

and phosphorus levels and bone mineralisation – from sunlight (see Chapter S – Sunshine).

➤ Selenium is a component of the master antioxidant glutathione, so you could say it's important (see Chapter A – Antioxidants) – found in Brazil nuts.

➤ Copper and zinc help with the production of glutathione – found in red meat and potatoes.

➤ Zinc supports our neural function, cellular renewal, restoration of cells, immune support and helps to reduce inflammation.

➤ Iron is essential for oxygen transport and energy metabolism – found in red meat and leafy greens.

➤ Calcium supports bone health and is essential for muscle contraction and nerve signalling – found in dairy.

FULVIC ACID

This is a special mention: fulvic acid molecules act as electron donors to our cellular membranes, so they support energy production and reduce oxidative cellular stress. Foods highest in fulvic acid will be those growing in healthy soils; though, where this is not possible, supplementing with fulvic acid is the best option.

> *'When you include fulvic acid, you have every known vitamin, every known mineral, every known amino acid, and all balanced by nature. It's a primary controller of cell membranes because it's one of the few substances that can be either plus or minus, as it needs to be. Hydrogen is the only other thing that can do that. Fulvic is also a great way to get rid of heavy metals as it can permeate the cell, grab the metals while the Fulvic pulls them out of the body.'*
>
> **Dr Jerry Tennant.**

The body needs nutrients to support itself so, where you can, select whole foods and avoid processed foods; but you also need to eat based on how you feel and sometimes you must eat what you can – something is often better than nothing. But, as a general rule, if it hasn't walked, flown, swum or grown from the ground, it is not food, and if you can't identify it or don't know what the ingredients are, then don't eat it.

This is a lot to take in, so don't feel like you need to make all the changes at once. Take it steadily, make small adjustments and be consistent to ensure solid foundations and sustainable change.

Live well; eat mindfully.

TOP TIPS

➤ Consume fresh, seasonal, organic, grass-fed whole foods.

➤ Choose unprocessed foods that are close to nature.

➤ Consume less sugar, junk foods, alcohol and caffeine.

➤ Consume a variety of foods – think colours, textures and flavours.

➤ Don't use supplementation at the expense of nutrient-dense foods.

➤ Be aware of food labels – make better-informed choices.

O – OILS

This chapter will help you if you:

➢ Want to know what essential oils are

➢ Want to know how to select essential oils

➢ Want top tips on how oils can support your wellness.

'Healing begins with an aromatic bath and daily massage.'

Hippocrates.

Essential oils have been used for many years. As far back as 100 AD, they have been noted as effective in relieving many ailments and issues. The use of essential oils was advocated by Hippocrates as the key to good health. As with anything, though, this needs to be done safely and under guidance.

Essential oils are extracted from plants through processes like distillation or cold pressing, which are the purest and most natural methods. The oils contain volatile chemical compounds or aromas.

When selecting an essential oil, it is not just about the scent, although something pleasing is preferable. It is also important to select food-grade therapeutic oils and know how the oil has been processed. Generally, these tend to be on the more expensive end of the scale, though they are safer for you as they do not involve chemical processing, adulterated or synthetic products. Essential oils are not all the same.

You should aim to avoid any essential oils that have been processed using solvent extraction methods. Unfortunately, this method is common throughout the 'perfume industry' and utilises chemicals such as acetone (an irritant) and hexane (a constituent of petroleum) to extract the oil. The plant materials are dissolved in the solvent and the chemicals then remain in the oil. These oils are found in lots of common items like soaps, hair products, air fresheners and fabric conditioners; however, they are synthetic and, as such, toxic to the body. It is always worth checking with labels and manufacturers.

Unfortunately, these accumulate in our systems over time and act as endocrine system disruptors that contribute to toxic overload, making our detoxification (see Chapter D – Detoxification) systems work hard trying to remove them and often manifesting in symptoms such as hormonal issues, thyroid issues, breathing disruption and headaches.

Finding pure essential oils to utilise for a fragrance in the home, as perfume/cologne, and in personal care and cleaning products is the best option for you and your family. As a guide, remember you shouldn't put anything on your skin that you wouldn't eat – your skin is your largest organ and semipermeable so it absorbs things topically.

The safest ways to utilise essential oils are through inhaling them and transdermal use.

The aromas in essential oils stimulate the olfactory system, which sends signals to the brain. The limbic system in the brain helps you to categorise each smell and recognise familiar scents and those which are pleasant versus those which are repulsive. This influences hormonal release based upon the emotions evoked by the fragrance, our memory of the scent and anything you have learned about the scent. For example, the smell of smoke indicates a fight/flight response. It bypasses our reasoning ability and is part of the immune system, trying to keep us alive by running from the fire. Nothing evokes memories as a smell does.

You can harness the positive effect upon the body by utilising comforting or pleasing aromas that promote a calming effect upon the parasympathetic nervous system (PNS) and help you to relax, rest and reset. Practising inhalation of the essential oils by using a diffuser in the room, or adding a few drops in a bowl of warm water and inhaling the steam, is a gentle method of use. When suffering from cold-like symptoms, diluting eucalyptus oil in warm water works fantastically as a decongestant, though caution should be taken to avoid irritation to the eyes.

You can also use essential oils topically, though it is a good idea to dilute these in a 'carrier oil', such as almond oil or fractionated coconut oil, or to add them to a warm bath. The compounds in the oils permeate the skin and are rapidly absorbed, with effects lasting from minutes to hours, depending upon the oils used. These are then expelled via our detoxification process. One of my personal favourites is to use lavender essential oil in fractionated coconut oil rubbed on the soles of my feet before bed, which promotes calm and restful sleep. Another great example is peppermint oil diluted in a carrier oil and applied to aching feet at the end of a long day – it is cooling, relaxing and rejuvenating.

The International Federation of Aromatherapists (IFA) recommends that oils are diluted by 0.5–5% and that a 2% dilution is generally safe for most healthy adults.

Essential oils can be used in place of your regular cleaning products for a non-toxic alternative if you are looking to reduce your exposure to environmental toxins in your home. For example, white vinegar, bicarbonate of soda and lemon oil makes a fantastic degreaser and all-purpose cleaner; just add it to a spray bottle. You can always add your favourite essential oils to alter the scent. Additionally, some brands sell Thieves Oil (Young Living) and On Guard (d☐Terra), which are great for combatting black mould.

If you are in any way unsure about which oils to choose or how to use them, please get in touch with a certified aromatherapist in your area. If you are struggling to locate one, please reach out to me and I will point you in the right direction – I am a certified aromatherapist, though not currently affiliated with a specific essential oil producer.

Please note that some oils should not be applied directly to the skin; and some, like citrus oils, should not be applied to the skin in direct sunlight; and some are contraindicated with certain health conditions and pregnancy – seek advice from a certified aromatherapy professional before use and take them under advisement. If you are overly sensitive to aromas, then using tinctures or infusions may be a preferable option as they are less volatile but still contain some of the active plant components. Also remember that some essential oils may not work for everyone, and it is best to make informed decisions by completing your own research and consulting with a professional aromatherapist.

TOP TIPS

➢ Source essential oils that are organic and produced via distillation and not through chemical processing.

➢ Take advice from a certified aromatherapist upon oil uses, combinations and any contraindications.

➢ Replace your regular perfume/cologne, air freshener, fabric conditioner and cleaning products with natural essential oils to help reduce your toxic load.

P − PRESENCE

This chapter will help you if you:

➤ Want to know more about presence/mindfulness

➤ Want to know how to become more self-aware

➤ Want top tips on how to practise being present/mindful.

Presence or mindfulness is paying attention by being in the present moment and doing it intentionally and without judgement. In other words, it's being aware and present in your experience.

Life can get super busy. Oftentimes, you get so caught up in your day-to-day that it can pass you by: sleep, eat, work, repeat.

Mindfulness meditation is a deliberate practice to help you regulate your attention by being present and in tune with your thoughts, emotions and body.

Mindfulness is being mindful of something. So when you drink your tea mindfully, it is called mindful drinking − you notice thoughts, emotions and the physical state of the body whilst drinking the tea; you are present with all of your senses and in the moment. When you walk mindfully, it is called mindful walking. And when you breathe mindfully, that is mindful breathing.

Mindfulness is the process of being in the moment and being present. The challenge is to re-establish ownership over your body and your mind. This means feeling free to know what you know and to feel what you feel without judgement and becoming calm and focussed.

Easier said than done sometimes.

The good thing is, you can practise being present and being mindful anywhere.

Mindful breathing is super simple – all you need to do is breathe. As you breathe, you become aware of your in-breath and out-breath. Simply allow your breath to take place. Notice the flow of breath.

Breathing through the nose is known as non-stressful breathing (see Chapter B – Breathing). This process brings your mind back to you; focussing on breathing allows your mind to focus, thus becoming mindful of your present state. As you breathe in, focus on the breath and the feeling of it moving in; as you breathe out, focus on the breath, and feel it moving out. The focus should stay on the breath and not on what you're having for dinner or what you're doing later on. The mental chatter should slow down and you can 'be'. You're no longer in the past, or in the future – you're right there in the present moment. You're not changing your breathing pattern but just maintaining the natural breath and aiming to follow the whole of the breath from the beginning. If your mind begins to wander, just bring your attention back to the breath, and be present.

Becoming aware of your body connects the body to the mind. So noticing any sensations in the body, or anything you feel, helps to relieve tension.

You can also be mindful when you are walking – allowing the breath to move naturally in an effortless way and with every step practising your intention of treading gently onto the earth, feeling what you can underneath your soles. There is no effort; you are in the moment, aware of all the sensations in your body, aware of your breath, aware of your environment, bringing your mind back to your body, feeling alive.

Mindful eating is about gaining more freedom around your food choices and becoming mindful about what you are putting into your body. A critical piece of the conversation often overlooked are the choices you make and the effects of these choices on yourself in the immediate situation and the bigger picture.

Making mindful food choices allows you to make better choices and reduces the stress in your relationship with food. Becoming aware that you have a choice about what you put into your body is a game-changer when it comes to your wellness. By savouring each moment you consume something, like chocolate or a glass of red wine, if you do it mindfully, it will help you avoid excess. Become mindful about what you eat and try adopting a new perspective that acts to empower you to take back control over your food choices. Start where you are and do you!

It doesn't just happen, though. It takes practice.

Consider a scenario where you are holding a glass of juice when someone comes along, bumps into you or shakes your arm and makes you spill. Ask yourself, 'Why did I spill the juice?' Your initial response will be, 'Well, because someone bumped into me, of course!' But take a look at this situation again. Really, you spilt the juice because there was juice in your glass. Had there been milk in the glass, you would have spilt milk. Whatever is inside the glass is what will spill out.

So, when life comes along and shakes you, which WILL inevitably happen, whatever is inside you will come out. So ask yourself, 'What's in my glass?' When life gets tough, what spills over? Joy, gratefulness, peace and humility? Or anger, bitterness, harsh words and reactions? You choose! This is how mindfulness can help.

Aim to fill your glass with gratitude, joy, kindness, gentleness and love for others.

Life is never always balanced... sh*t happens that disrupts our plans; it is all about the ebbs and flows; but you gotta ride the waves and it doesn't matter if you're a pro surfer or scared of water... sh*t still happens!

'We convince by our presence.'

Walt Whitman

TOP TIPS

Here is a way you can practise becoming more mindful of yourself. Try a simple body scan:

➢ Get into a comfortable position with a straight back but not tense.

➢ Close your eyes.

➢ Tune into your body – breathe through the nose.

➢ Notice how the body feels.

➢ Start at the top of your head and slowly move downwards to the feet and notice any areas of tension.

➢ Now imagine those areas relaxing.

Q – QUALITY OVER QUANTITY

This chapter will help you if you:

➤ Want to know the difference between quantity and quality

➤ Want to know how quality affects you

➤ Want top tips on how you can add more quality to your life.

Quality is a characteristic or a feature such as durability or friendliness, and quantity refers to the numerical value of something such as a price or number of.

Quality is a subjective marker, meaning that it is personal to the individual's perception, just like when you say 'the beauty is in the eye of the beholder', whereas quantity is something that can be directly compared.

Moving your attention from quantity to quality can be a game-changer. You are allowing yourself to select the best option for you. Choosing quality is a good rule to live by if you are looking to make more conscious and sustainable decisions in life.

Placing your focus upon quality rather than quantity can provide you with a better life experience as it offers you more relevance. So, rather than focussing on vanity metrics and numerical values, the emphasis is upon depth, meaning and substance.

You may save yourself money and promote sustainability by investing in quality items since they will last longer and have less need for replacement and thus offer a better return on investment. The phrase 'buy cheap and buy twice' comes to mind.

Having a large quantity of things causes you to be distracted as there are more options and choices involved. This can lead you to become overwhelmed and stressed. Having fewer items that are higher quality means there is more headspace because less of it is used for memory and cognitive decision making, leaving time for the important stuff and helping you to focus upon significant things instead of everything.

Choosing quality initially requires you to be more selective, though in the long term, it reduces the choice overload and enhances your ability to make better decisions.

Quality often brings feelings of contentment, though you don't always get that dopamine hit you may feel from the instant gratification of large quantities of stuff. However, there is more focus on your values and the things that matter to you over any short-term satisfaction. It is playing the long game.

By selecting quality, you will care more about the things, connections and activities you have invested in following more thought and time involved in their selection. You are then more likely to appreciate, place a higher value on, care, nurture for and look after them. These are the assets and resources that you have taken time and energy to invest in. The way that you care for others and your belongings is a reflection of your self-care and value of yourself. By saving for and investing in something of high quality, you are more likely to enjoy the purchase.

This not only applies to items and purchases but people too. If you surround yourself with quality people, they will support, uplift and nourish you, often merely by being in their presence. (see Chapter E – Energy; review radiators and drains). These are high-quality people that resonate with positive vibes. So, if you need to upgrade your social circle or your clients, remember your vibe attracts your tribe – by changing your intentions and what you are putting out into the universe, the universal law of attraction states that this is what you will attract towards you. To up-level the quality you are surrounded by, consider your dominant habitual thoughts and how these cause you to feel. If they're not what you are looking for, then write down what you want to attract and how it will make you feel. There you go – the recipe for up-levelling your circle. Social influence means you are more similar to the people you choose to associate with, so seek those who naturally resonate with you.

It isn't about the quantity; it's the quality that has the most profound influence upon you. High-quality connections, interactions and relationships provide substance on and above the surface-level pleasantries. When you cease seeking any form of approval from others and choose quality for yourself, you are letting go of the need for external validation and embracing your own value.

> *'You are the average of the five people you spend the most time with.'*
>
> **Jim Rohn.**

Consider the nutrient density of the foods you consume and the water you drink and whether they are nourishing you, supporting your energy levels and supporting your wellness (as opposed to illness) – rather than merely considering the quantity of food you consume. Eating smaller portions of higher quality nutritious food will support your wellness, satiety and enjoyment of the food.

By placing your emphasis, energy and time on high quality, you are completing an act of self-care by conserving your precious resources for the important things that matter to you. Inviting quality into your life is the equivalent of telling yourself, 'You're worth it, you deserve it; you deserve the best.'

Focussing on quality reduces the need for superficial things and allows you to instead search for the depth, meaning and value offered. You can apply the quality over quantity principle to all areas of your life, including things, your career, your social life, your connections and relationships, the media you consume and the people you surround yourself with. Quality improves wellness when you focus on the areas that contribute the most to life. Quality ALWAYS adds more value.

Quality reduces distractions from your overarching intentions and goals. Instead of chasing time or volume, focussing upon quality helps you to prioritise things in life rather than having everything all at once.

There is lots of 'stuff' going on that vies for your attention; choosing to select quality over quantity will allow you to be far more discerning of what you spend your time on and whom you spend your time with. Choosing to create a better life is you valuing yourself and making one quality decision after the other.

The route to bringing more quality into your life is to raise your standards and make conscious choices. This is not a quick fix; it is a process that starts with you valuing yourself. When you can see your worth, you allow yourself to choose quality, from the people in your life to the relationships you have, to the activities you undertake, to the books you read, to the purchases you make. You are levelling up.

'Quality is never an accident; it is always the result of intelligent efforts.'

John Ruskin.

TOP TIPS

➤ Make a list of where you can add value to your life by choosing quality over quantity. Consider areas like friendships, relationships, food choices, how you make a living, etc.

➤ Make one conscious decision to change one thing; for example, what you will eat for breakfast – will it be a full English or will you opt for a smoothie packed full of phytonutrients?

➤ Rinse and repeat. Select another area where you wish to add value and make a quality decision. It is simply making one quality decision after the other.

R – RESILIENCE

This chapter will help you if you:

➤ Want to know what resilience is

➤ Want to know how you become resilient

➤ Want top tips on how to practise resilience.

'You, me, or nobody is gonna hit as hard as life.
But it ain't about how hard ya hit. It's about
how hard you can get hit and keep moving forward.
How much you can take and keep moving forward.
That's how winning is done!'

Sylvester Stallone, Rocky Balboa.

This quote sums up resilience perfectly.

The number of stressors that you encounter daily is increasing, from your internal self-imposed pressures, to your environment, work and family life demands. You are being pushed into imbalances and that takes a lot of our energy and resources.

When life is good, it seems as though things are easy; it just flows, the sun shines, it feels as though everything is going your way and you are just living your best life.

Then sh*t happens. Like you, I've been there too. Honestly, when the rug gets pulled from underneath you, sometimes you simply come crashing down. Other times, it feels like the momentum has flipped you around in the air and landed you on your head.

This is where resilience comes in.

Your inner drive and ability to remain optimistic will certainly support you when you feel you are up against it. If you can remain positive and believe you can change track and find an alternative solution to your challenges, it will help you keep moving forwards. Even if it is only one step, it is one step closer. Oftentimes, it is about looking at the opportunities a challenging situation may create and becoming solution-focussed because searching for and then applying solutions is what helps you to progress.

Whatever you are passionate about is your 'why'. It's something you may lose sight of on occasion, but knowing your 'why' is important. When things get tough, honestly going back to your why is often what helps you to push on.

> *'Our greatest weakness lies in giving up. The most certain way to succeed is always to try just one more time.'*
> **Thomas Edison.**

Resilience can also be noted as your ability to get back to equilibrium as effectively and efficiently as possible; essentially, it is the ability to bridge the gap between functioning well, and the ability to just about function.

When things do go awry, trying to focus on your whole reason for doing something and the process it involves is key to resilience, even when your brain is trying to make you give up because things are challenging or the outcome looks bleak. Skills that you can discover through any challenges or knock-backs can become powerful lessons and assets to support your winning in the future. It may not feel like it as you are going through it, but upon reflection, you'll likely note your growth and development, along with other skills you have acquired.

Of course, there are times when you can go it alone and get through things. Though sometimes you need others in the form of support, encouragement, mentorship or as a reminder to take a time out.

'No man is an island, entire of itself.'

John Donne.

This is a time to call upon the positive relationships you have and those who cheer you on, elevate and ground you. These supportive relationships are ones to nurture now for the future.

It can often be difficult to recognise there are times you need others to help – even more so to ask for help. Perhaps you feel like you should know what to do or how to deal with things or that you're not worthy of help, care or support. But, if you carry all the responsibility, it mounts up and there may come a point where it is just too much to cope with.

Sometimes you may just think, 'What's the point?' This is when you need to stop and breathe. Take a time out and regroup.

Then, take another step. This is when you become resilient – when you move when you didn't think you could. It may be something as simple as putting one foot in front of the other, sending an email or picking up the phone. You can do this. It is important to manage challenges to maintain your mental, physical and soulful wellness.

Please, if you are struggling, reach out.

When you are faced with a challenge or a setback, it is far too easy to feel angry or resentful and to adopt a negative frame of mind. But, as my mum has always said, the person this hurts most is you. So stop. Reframe the situation and change your perspective.

Taking action, even just changing your thoughts, can provide you with a focus. Don't let negative thoughts take charge. Your mindset plays a vital role in your resilience. Don't sit with negative thoughts and let them fester; take action to get them out of your head. The more action you can take, the more support and care you are providing yourself. Nourishing your body, mind and soul will help you to develop a deeper connection with yourself and boost your ability to be resilient.

You can't do all the things all the time. At some point, your body will simply say 'no' and this will manifest as symptoms such as pain, dysfunction, brain fog and fatigue. Recovery is not a quick fix. So it is better to recognise that you need assistance and have a network available, whether this is in the form of emotional support, business support, your mindset or your physical wellness; have some options in place. Additionally, having an 'emergency' plan or outline that you can default to when you are not at your best is helpful.

A great question to ask yourself is, 'Is this serving me?' It's one I ask a lot. If something isn't working for your greater good, then consider your options.

If it all does go wrong and if the proverbial sh*t does hit the fan, you are allowed to acknowledge this. You are allowed to feel sh*t. You are allowed to feel sorry for yourself. But only for a short while. Limit yourself to 10–15 minutes. Put a timer on your phone if you need to, but then, that's it.

> *'The problem with pity parties is very few people come,*
> *and those who do don't bring presents.'*
>
> **Zig Ziglar.**

Then decide you will do something to move yourself forwards. Remember, DON'T make big decisions when you are emotional. Come back to them once the emotions have settled.

There is always a positive to be found – ALWAYS. The challenge is often finding it even when it feels negative. If you need to, write it down; now focus on this aspect.

And above all, be proud of yourself, and judge yourself a little less.

> *'You have been criticising yourself for years,*
> *and it hasn't worked. Try approving of yourself*
> *and see what happens.'*
>
> **Louise Hay.**

You are also unique, so don't compare your situation to another's – there is no comparison. The reality is that only you know your own problems. Your life experiences have likely prepared you for managing your situation; how you cope becomes habitual.

TOP TIPS

➤ Take the time to pause, reflect and ask yourself, 'Is this serving me?'

➤ Draw on your previous experiences and ask for support when you need it.

➤ Learn to recognise the signs within and have strategies in place to support yourself.

➤ From calming meditations, blocking your negative thoughts, positive affirmations, to talking with friends, whatever it is, implement it.

S – SUNSHINE

This chapter will help you if you:

➢ Want to know the importance of sunshine

➢ Want to know how sunshine affects you

➢ Want top tips on how to get enough sunshine.

'Ô, Sunlight! The most precious gold to be found on Earth.'

Roman Payne.

Sunshine is a wonderful thing. It's so wonderful that you need the full solar spectrum to remain well and for optimal health. Plus it feels good and has an essential role in energising you. The sun is your life force.

Sunlight has different frequencies of the visible light spectrum that are detected by the human eye, including red, orange, yellow, green, blue and violet. Each of the frequencies of sunlight provides the master clock in your brain with specific signals. These signals control the release of various hormones and neurotransmitters (messengers) that signal to every cell in the body at different times of the day. This influences your circadian rhythms (see Chapter C – Circadian rhythms).

Morning light is mostly IR (infrared) light and from the very first light of the day, the photoreceptors in your eyes and skin detect the light frequencies. In the eyes, the light signals travel through the optic nerve to the clock in the brain which halts melatonin secretion, so your melatonin levels begin to fall and cortisol begins to rise within 30 minutes of waking up. At around 7 am, cortisol and your blood pressure are at their highest, which increases blood flow in preparation for the day. This morning light also signals the production of melatonin in the pineal gland, which is stored for release after dark (see Chapter Z – Zzzz: sleep) and also initiates dopamine production to support our mental health and cognition.

Heliotherapy dates back to the ancient Greeks in Helios. Even Florence Nightingale used it with her patients. The sun essentially irradiates the blood, with UV sunlight stimulating red blood cell production and coordinating the white blood cells' immune response. When sensed by the skin, sunlight increases venous oxygen, lowers blood pressure and can support the immune function in the gut and respiratory system.

Your skin needs to be exposed to sunlight without sunscreen to synthesise vitamin D. Vitamin D is the result of sunlight interacting with low-density lipoprotein (LDL) cholesterol in the skin and the intracellular water made by your mitochondria (during energy production) when it is activated by the infrared (IR) light from the sun (UVB). Vitamin D is then converted to its circulating form in the liver and then to a bio-available useable form in the kidneys; magnesium helps to support this process in the kidneys. Therefore, looking after your liver and kidney health is essential! Also, dehydrated skin cells cannot produce vitamin D even if they are exposed to sunlight, so hydration is key.

Vitamin D is also classed as more of a hormone in its function than a 'vitamin' as it is synthesised from cholesterol, just like our other hormones. If you are 'deficient' in vitamin D, the likelihood is it is not a vitamin D issue; rather, your hormones are likely out of balance – remember, they're made from cholesterol. Hormones work together; they are the chemical messengers in the body that regulate many processes. Most of this starts with the retina of the eye in response to sunlight. So, if you have low vitamin D, chances are you don't sleep well, have digestive issues, hormonal dysfunction and maybe fertility concerns.

To generate vitamin D from the sun, you need to be in the sunlight when it is around 36 degrees from the horizon; this means sometime between 11 and 4 pm. Take a look at the pavement and see when your shadow is shorter than you are. You can also check out the D-minder app that helps to find the best timing for your location.

If you are exposed to the sun and cannot make vitamin D, it is most likely your light/dark environment and artificial light that are impairing this process. A week's worth of sun exposure can enable you to store enough vitamin D for the whole winter, so it is likely not a sun problem. You can use the pointers in Chapter C – Circadian rhythms, and see if that makes a difference. In the short term, you can support vitamin D.

When your vitamin D levels are low, your mitochondria release light (energy); the more energy that is released means your cells can't work properly and that leads to poor oxygen utilisation, which increases oxidative stress (see Chapter A – Antioxidants) and inflammation. Vitamin D also helps regulate adrenaline, noradrenaline and dopamine production in the brain and helps to protect from serotonin depletion. When vitamin D is low in the gut, the tight junctions in the gut wall open, creating a 'leaky gut', which also affects serotonin production. Therefore, when vitamin D is low, there is an increased risk of low mood.

Exposing your eyes and skin to artificial light lowers melatonin, which impairs the mitochondrial ability to make the intracellular water you need to make vitamin D. This also impairs the 100Hz cellular frequency needed by mitochondria for fat burning during sleep. So your light environment does matter (see Chapter C – Circadian rhythms).

Light is life. Life supports life. When the light from the sun is absorbed in the form of light energy, in the life that you consume, this comes from live energetic enzymes found in live whole plant foods that feed your cells. Vitamin D is a fat-soluble vitamin so you can also gain this when you consume healthy fats and have a great digestive process to absorb vitamin D. Grass-fed meats, grass-fed butter, organic eggs, avocados and olives are a great start! Supplementation is not usually necessary in the summer months for most, unless you are immune-suppressed or ill. So get out in the sunshine, lovelies.

By exposing your skin to UV light, you can also influence your metabolism of fat because all food is broken down into electrons and protons and is fed through the mitochondrial electron transport chain – meaning you gain energy from sunlight! Sunlight charges water in the body like a battery; essentially, the photons of light (light particles) are converted to electrons for energy in your body. Light frequencies are measured in nanometers; each photon's energy is in proportion with its frequency so the energy is relative to its frequency.

Photons from sunlight are captured by the aromatic amino acids (AAs) in tyrosine, which your cells use to create dopamine. You also do the same with tryptophan once the light hits the AAs in your cells to make melatonin/serotonin. This enhances blood circulation and nutrient and oxygen delivery.

Early morning sunlight increases melanin in the eyes, skin and hair, and the more melanin you have, the more sunlight energy you can collect. This also builds your solar callous, which protects you from sunburn. Lack of sun exposure decreases the production of melanin in the eyes, skin and hair. This decreases the efficiency of the body to use sunlight to create energy so your mitochondria have adapted if you have lighter eyes, skin, and hair.

Everything emits energy. You emit light energy from your interconnected energy fields to your biophotons. You are beings of light and light emits energy. So you see that light is life!

TOP TIPS

➢ The absolute best thing to do is have regular exposure to the sun on your bare skin, without sunscreen, for at least 30 minutes a day. Morning and afternoon are good times.

➢ Avoid the midday sun if you are sensitive (morning and evening sun are best to get used to the sun and build your 'solar callous' to reduce sensitivity and reduce burning risk, or they can serve as a good alternative if you remain sensitive).

➢ Support yourself with whole-food nutrition.

➢ Get your vitamin D levels checked (see reference section).

T – THOUGHTS

This chapter will help you if you:

- ➤ Want to know the importance of your thoughts
- ➤ Want to know how your thoughts influence your wellness
- ➤ Want top tips on how to change your thoughts.

Your thoughts are important. They have a direct influence upon your physical, mental and spiritual health. You have approximately 60–100,000 thoughts every day. That's a lot of thinking.

A positive thought resonates at a higher frequency than a negative thought, so positive thoughts are essentially more powerful. Research demonstrates that positive thinking can be used to effectively prevent anxiety.

However, you are programmed with negative bias so positive thoughts take more practice.

What are your thoughts right now? Just sit there and take a moment to consider. Are your thoughts best serving you?

Did you know that thoughts affect things? There is a saying: 'What you think about you bring about.' When you put a thought out there, it has an energy attached to it and every thought you have emits a frequency; this creates resonance and attaches an energy to it. When you put it out there, you are attracting it to you. Essentially, what you think about, you draw towards you – so every thought you put out there comes back to you.

'If you realised how powerful your thoughts are,
you would never think a negative thought.'

Peace Pilgrim.

Your energy is also directly affected and influenced by your thoughts. The thoughts you think relative to everything – money, relationships, home, business or whatever – resonate at specific frequencies and send out these vibrations into your environment. This brings to you the people and circumstances that surround you.

Everything that comes to you is about what you've got going on vibrationally and the thoughts and frequencies you are emitting into the world. Oftentimes, what you have going on vibrationally is because of what you are observing; so be careful what you surround yourself with!

All things in our universe are constantly in motion and in process. Even objects that appear to be stationary are vibrating, oscillating and resonating at specific frequencies. You could say that what you think about, you feel, and what you feel, you attract. Thoughts are viewed as electromagnetic representations of nerve activity. So thoughts are electric; when an emotion is attached, it gives off that thought energy and becomes magnetic so emotions are magnetic too. You are attracting the frequencies you emit.

If the brain uses upwards of 20% of all the energy in our bodies, and if you are using this to produce negative thoughts, you are attaching a lot of energy to them and hence attracting negative thoughts to you. Lots of negative thoughts and self-talk affect your health since you are lowering your cellular vibration; but you can counteract this by being mindful of your thoughts. If you catch yourself being overly negative or critical, then you should stop and think of something positive. In this way, you are interrupting the pattern of your thoughts.

What you think about, you feel; what you feel, you attract.

Thoughts are electric.

Emotions are magnetic.

Be the kind of magnet you want to be.

You have trillions of cells, and your cells are covered in thousands of antennae that act as receptors that resonate with specific frequencies. Your thoughts and emotions are directly influenced by the environment you are in; this environment creates signals that resonate with your antennae – the stronger the emotion attached to the thought, the stronger the signal and physiological response. This is great for something like love because that release of oxytocin, serotonin and dopamine feels gooood. However, with something like fear, your defence systems are activated – hello cortisol, adrenaline and inflammatory markers – which initially and temporarily decrease your immunity. If, however, this fear is prolonged, it makes you more prone to illness and dysfunction.

Having an 'attitude of gratitude' and being grateful influences our vibration. Sometimes it may feel difficult to find things to be grateful for, but when you flip your perspective, you often find there is much to be grateful for. When you start being thankful for things, you open the door to higher vibrations and positive things happening.

By looking within and considering the story you are telling yourself through your thought patterns and choices, you can have a huge impact on your health outcomes simply by changing the way you think.

'Once you replace negative thoughts with positive ones, you'll start having positive results.'

Willie Nelson.

You are part of your human experience, which is influenced by your thoughts and feelings, and can elicit an illusory state. This state can either be a source of confinement, or a source of inspiration to broaden your horizons.

TOP TIPS

There's a really easy way you can do this to counteract what you perceive as a not-so-great day:

➢ Once you get into bed and before you go to sleep, think of three things you are grateful for and feel how grateful you are.

➢ These can be people, places, talents, the day's events, physical things – by being grateful, you are thinking positively and changing that thought pattern and this causes an emotive response.

➢ Emotions are literally energy in motion. By having an emotional response, you attach more weight to it; this then acts as a magnet and you attract similar frequencies to you. Heard of raising your vibration? This is it!

U – UNWIND

This chapter will help you if you:

➢ Want to know the importance of unwinding

➢ Want to know the effects of unwinding

➢ Want top tips on how to unwind to support your wellness.

'The time to relax is when you don't have time for it.'

Sydney Harris.

Needing to unwind is becoming increasingly common, although your normal state of being is to be at ease, relaxed and with abundant energy flow.

Unfortunately, you often don't feel this way.

Your emotions and the feelings they cause govern our bodies' innate hierarchy of priorities when it comes to your wellness and overall ability to relax.

Have you ever been sitting at home when a negative notion entered your mind? Something that triggered you to feel unappreciated, frustrated, jealous or angry? Just by having this notion or thought, an emotion is always attached and that causes you to ruminate (see Chapter T – Thoughts).

This thought process then triggers events in the body which cause the nervous system to feel unsafe so it cannot let its guard down. Your body enters survival mode and the stress response goes on high alert – into fight or flight mode – leaving you unable to relax and continually feeling wired, tired or both.

In order to relax, your nervous system needs to feel safe and return to equilibrium; it needs to tone down the sympathetic nervous system (SNS) response and turn on the relaxation response of the parasympathetic nervous system (PNS).

Taking a time out isn't just reserved for sports teams or naughty children. Taking time for yourself is important. Using this time to unwind, decompress and recharge your batteries is imperative to your wellness. Even 10 minutes is better than nothing. Yes, 10 minutes where you stop, without any distractions, turn off your phone, lock yourself in the bathroom if you have to – but 10 minutes where you do nothing! Lying on the bed in a dark room is beneficial; it only takes 10 minutes and you will feel recharged. You can practise your breathing (see Chapter B – Breathing) to help calm your system.

You can make a conscious effort to relax your mind. Rather than trying to force an idea, simply let go and allow your inner insight and intuition to awaken. Meditation and breathwork are great tools to support the manifestation of creative ideas. When your mind is relaxed and has space, just like when you are daydreaming, you can often get a lot of awareness. Just breathe in and let it go.

Another way you can do this is by considering your tongue. You read that correctly – more so, though, it's the position of your tongue.

The muscles of the tongue are controlled by the twelfth cranial nerve or hypoglossal nerve. This arises from the part of the brain stem called the medulla oblongata, which connects to the spinal cord, and governs several involuntary functions like breathing, heart function, digestion, sneezing and swallowing. The position of your tongue influences the whole body. If your tongue is positioned on the roof of your mouth, this stimulates your vagus nerve (the tenth cranial nerve) and activates the PNS. This elicits a relaxation response, supports nasal breathing and supports your neck or cervical spine. So keeping the tongue in a relaxed position has a calming effect on your body and your mind.

Your posture also has an effect upon your ability to relax and, believe it or not, is linked to the position of your tongue also! If you want to relax, you need to find ways to take the stress out of the body. Try standing or sitting up straight with your shoulders back and relaxed. Look up at the sky or close your eyes and turn them to look upwards at your third eye (mid-forehead). Bring into your mind the thought of something beautiful or an experience you loved. Then smile – this is important. Turn the corners of your mouth upwards. Feel the feels. It is impossible not to relax when you smile.

Your environment affects your mood so surrounding yourself with disorganised, cluttered, dirty workspaces will lower your vibration and your mood and increase your stress levels. You become accepting of what you see; therefore, surround yourself with things that enhance your mood and help you vibrate at a higher frequency. So tidy up and get organised. It's amazing how much better you feel after a spring clean!

Find time to 'chill out' and relax daily as becoming over-stressed is not good for the immune system so finding ways to unwind and mindfully relax is important. Blocking space out in your day, every day, where you are still, quiet and notice your thoughts; practising nasal diaphragmatic breathing; listening to music; reading; walking in nature; moving/exercising and simply stopping are all forms of meditation.

By using your time wisely and allowing yourself to unwind and recharge, you can reach decisions with better clarity and let go of fear surrounding things that are important to you.

'It's a good idea always to do something relaxing prior to making an important decision in your life.'

Paulo Coelho.

TOP TIPS

➤ Block out time to unwind in your daily calendar. Often this is a good idea at the start or the end of the day.

➤ Find the way to unwind that suits you the best. If it helps, you can make a list to have at hand and select one from the list each day.

➤ Realise that unwinding, decompressing, rest, relaxation and recharging are all necessary for your wellness and for optimal function.

V – VISUALISATION

This chapter will help you if you:

➤ Want to know what visualisation is

➤ Want to know how to use visualisation

➤ Want top tips on how to practise visualisation.

'Visualisation is daydreaming with a purpose.'

Bo Bennett.

Visualisation is also known as mental imagery or mental rehearsal and plays a significant role in your wellness, since what you imagine influences your reality. You will have experienced this if you have ever watched a scary or action-packed film, then gone to bed and replayed the scenes in your mind; your body responds in exactly the same ways as if you were experiencing it.

The good news is that visualisation is a technique that can be used to your advantage to support your physical, mental and soulful wellness and can be practised, refined and used in many ways.

When practising visualisation or mental imagery, you utilise a cognitive process for producing motor actions or movements. It is a technique widely used by athletes to enhance performance, which many research studies have confirmed the positive effects of. You can try this to boost your own performance in life.

When you visualise or imagine something, you are choosing a conscious action that uses the same areas of the brain involved in literally performing something as if you had taken part in the action. So you could say that the brain can't differentiate between what is done and what is imagined.

Whenever you imagine something and get engrossed in that imaginational state, feeling all the feels as though it were real – that's when you are creating or recreating. This is when your thoughts essentially become your reality. An action or state – whether real or imagined and when linked with your emotions, feelings and intentions – has great power and you can choose to harness this power.

The more you visualise something, the more you formulate an image of your future actions and behaviour, which will be easier for you to undertake. You are creating neural pathways that fire in unison and your brain is creating a multi-dimensional experience for you – your brain has already experienced something and is preparing for your future.

When you are using visualisations, you can adopt different perspectives: either experience something as though you are watching yourself or as though you are participating in a task. This is termed external visualisation where you are picturing yourself from outside of your body, like watching yourself in a film or walking through the route before the race. Or it can be internal where you are imagining yourself performing an activity and simulating the feelings involved (sight, smell, hearing, touch, taste).

The visualisations capture the 'feeling' or 'emotion' of the experience. Whether you are creating or recreating an experience, it takes you to another place.

So why does mental imagery/visualisation work?

The brain is unable to distinguish between a real experience and an imagined experience. Studies have detected the underlying processes in the brain, including 'brain waves' during actual movements and mental imagery, through neuro-imaging using EEG (electroencephalography), PET scans (positron emission tomography) and MRI scans (magnetic resonance imaging). Therefore, imagery can be deemed as the 'functional equivalence' of actual movement. The brain sends impulses via the CNS (central nervous system) to the peripheral nervous system and you may see muscle twitches, etc., as the brain creates motor-neural pathways.

Visualisations can be used for:

➢ management of the mind
➢ mental rehearsal
➢ relaxation
➢ developing confidence
➢ enhancing concentration.

So how can you perform visualisations?

Firstly, you need to be in a calm state, so oftentimes a period of brief meditation can be beneficial prior to visualising (see Chapter P – Presence). You initially want to practise linking the heart to the brain so you 'feel' your images. A great way to do this is to practise your breathing meditation for a couple of weeks by following the breath and noticing how you feel.

Once you have done this and you can calm the mind, you can move into visualising. Again, tagging this onto the meditation practice is a great move. You can imagine the heart glowing in a bright light that is filling up the body and then imagine the brain with the same light. Do this for a couple of weeks to help connect the brain and the heart – your mind and emotions.

Now you are ready to get more emotional. This helps to anchor the visualisation experience and make it realistic. Visualise what you want. Focus on the image and how it makes you feel. Allow the feeling to wash over you. Consider what you can see, what you can hear, what you can smell, what you can touch, what you can taste and what you can feel. This is integrating the mind, body and soul.

By using mental imagery, you are bridging the space between who you are and the image of who you will be and how you show up in the world.

So you can create change by practising visualisation attached to feelings and emotions; your brain automatically creates an image of what you want.

'Meditate, visualise and create your own reality and the universe will simply reflect back to you.'

Amit Ray.

TOP TIPS

➢ Calm the mind with breathing meditation.

➢ Start by visualising the environment in full technicolour and be clear with the details. The more vivid the image is, the more the brain accepts it and the more real it feels.

➤ Imagine the scene so clearly that you feel your mood changing. Engage all your senses; focus completely on what you can sense and how it is making you feel.

➤ Then, rinse and repeat daily!

W – WATER

This chapter will help you if you:

- ➢ Want to know the importance of quality water
- ➢ Want to know how water affects you
- ➢ Want top tips on how to get quality water.

Water is super important and is one of the five elements for a good reason.

Hydration is more than just about your water intake, though water is the first place to start when it comes to health and wellness. Without enough water in your body systems, they become stagnant; the natural flow in charge of distributing nutrients and removing waste products is disrupted and toxins build up. You are approximately 70% water so a lack of fluid leads to an accumulation of metabolic waste, which can further lead to compromises in both your physical and mental wellness and, subsequently, your quality of life.

When you are well hydrated, this supports your natural detoxification pathways, lymphatic flow and drainage, and helps to remove pathogens and other waste materials. Hydration is a key element in maintaining a healthy immune system. Your immune system is highly dependent on the nutrients in your bloodstream and your bloodstream is made mostly of fluid with your blood plasma being 93% water. Thus, sufficient water is needed to properly transport oxygen and vital nutrients to each organ system.

Obviously, you need water, but many variables can affect this.

Water supports many of your body's functions by improving oxygen delivery to cells, transporting nutrients, flushing toxins and supporting natural healing processes. Dehydration slows this process down and can contribute to muscular tension, headaches, low serotonin production, poor sleep and digestive issues. A loss of 1% water impairs our thermoregulatory processes and can impair cognitive performance.

Water contains minerals or electrolytes that are essentially salts composed of positively and negatively charged ions. These ions transfer electrical messages across your cells for them to function. Every cell has a semi-permeable membrane, meaning that it lets certain things in and out of the cell including water, nutrients and waste products. Hydrating with clean water is important for healthy kidneys and filtration as your renal system maintains your electrolyte balance so long as there is sufficient water available. When you are dehydrated and/or deficient in minerals, this makes your kidneys work harder just to filter and excrete waste. So adequate hydration also requires minerals for the water to be absorbed into cells.

One of the ways you become dehydrated at a cellular level is when you are not seeing morning sunlight or you have too much blue light in the evenings. This negatively affects your vitamin D production, along with your oestrogen, testosterone and progesterone levels as the mitochondria cannot work efficiently if they are dehydrated. As a consequence, you can experience low libido, reduced oxytocin (our pleasure hormone), poor quality sleep, and poor recovery and restoration.

There appear to be widely accepted recommendations when it comes to water consumption, such as to drink half your body weight in water (oz), eight glasses or two litres a day, so it's quite confusing to know what to do. To be honest, though, it depends upon your overall health status, what else you're consuming and what you are doing to enhance dehydration, such as being in a humid environment and/or excessive sweating.

What is the BEST water to drink?

> water that is unpolluted – free of chemicals and contamination

> water that carries a living signature

> water that has a balanced and coherent set of minerals.

You need to drink water to sustain health. You are water-based so sourcing your water should be high up on your list of priorities to support your wellness.

In an ideal scenario, your water would be in its most natural form from a spring – clean, untouched and unpolluted – living water. However, the realities for most of us are far from this. You should also consider the water you use to feed the plants, vegetables and fruits you consume and the water you provide for your pets.

Natural springwater contains minerals, which you need at a cellular level to maintain many of the actions, interactions and reactions that create our energy and keep your body well. However, shop-bought mineral and springwaters are a little different – scrutinise the labels as to the content and also consider that plastic bottles may leach chemicals into the water. However, shop-bought water is still a superior alternative to tap water. Also remember that minerals are bound to carbon in naturally carbonated springwater, which helps with delivery into your cells, whereas with artificially carbonated water, the minerals are not bound and it depletes our cells of minerals. This is a huge consideration when you think about bone density.

Your next best option for tap water is a filter that removes the chemicals and nasties you don't want to be consuming, especially fluoride and chlorine. Or use a water distiller, which does strip the water of everything, though it may help if the body is heavily toxic. Distilled water is a safe alternative because it has no added processes or chemicals and you can structure it by adding minerals back in in the form of a pinch of sea salt or as fulvic acid or vortexing.

Structured water is life. It's not just the quality or quantity of water; it's the structure that's most important. Structured water is living water and it's known as the fourth phase of water (G. Pollack). You can find it in nature when you see moving water across streams and rocks where the constant flow creates oxygen. When you drink this type of water, it's viscous to your cells meaning it is not quite a solid and is ionic. It is negative ion water and that helps support our body in removing free radicals and stabilising positive ions. Frozen water has the same structure as structured water.

Light and water interact in the mitochondria to hydrate us at a cellular level. Our cells contain water with a specific crystalline molecular structure and function that allows them to behave like batteries; the water absorbs sunlight and the electrons in water collect photons to deliver them to the mitochondria. If you are dehydrated, you lose the ability to harness the sun's photons to stimulate the electrons in your blood plasma and recharge your cellular battery. You can place your water in the sun to charge. If your water is placed in Miron glass, this only allows violet, ultraviolet (UV) and infrared photons to penetrate it, blocking every other frequency of visible light. Visible purple light has the highest frequency of all colours of visible light, and it activates and balances the molecular structure of organisms.

TOP TIPS

➤ Drink cleaner water. Get a water filter (a Berkey gravity filter, a distiller or reverse osmosis) or gather water yourself from a spring or well for free.

➤ Remineralise your water where necessary, especially if it is distilled. Vortex your water and add fulvic minerals.

➤ Drink enough water for your needs. As a guide, for most people, in ounces, drink half your body weight.

X – X-FACTOR

This chapter will help you if you:

➢ Want to know what an X-factor is

➢ Want to know if you have an X-factor

➢ Want top tips on how to identify your X-factor.

'If you haven't found it yet, keep looking.'

Steve Jobs.

What makes you *you?*

When you think of the answer, what comes to mind? Is it what you have learned, your achievements, family or your social circle?

It's everything about you from your values, beliefs and characteristic traits to your super 'special' skills and abilities.

So what is your X-factor?

Your X-factor is what makes you special. And every one of you is special in your own way.

Your X-factor is something that fills you with joy. When you are applying your X-factor, things seem to flow with ease. You begin to feel, see and do things differently. You seem to have up-levelled and upgraded to a different realm and level of consciousness. You are shining your light.

Now you just have to work out exactly what your X-factor is.

You have a unique life story. Take a moment right now and allow yourself to explore in your own mind the moments in your life that have helped shape who you are today. There will be many but you will have stand-out points so the simplest way to start is to write these down. Finding your X-factor means being consciously curious and exploring your associations with your life, your passions and what makes you you.

When you are looking inwards at yourself, remember you are unique. Consider the skills and abilities you are highly proficient in, those you have developed and that make your heart happy when you use them. These are your 'special' abilities – the ones that cause you to feel fully present, self-fulfilled and happy.

Once you start doing this, you are part way to discovering your X-factor!

Next, write down your experiences, your goals, your interests and your passions. Then look at all your achievements and what you have accomplished throughout the course of your life and write them down too. Include all the things that have happened, grown and developed throughout your life.

Then record yourself talking about how you did it – how you did the things you did. For example, you lost 10 lbs in three months by eating well, reducing your stress, moving more and meditating for mindfulness. This demonstrates your commitment and consistency amongst other skillsets. The next and most important step is to listen back to the recording; this helps to pinpoint your 'special' abilities. This may seem like the most difficult part but just take out your phone and start recording yourself.

The thing is, your 'special' abilities are likely automatic so you need to seek help with the next part. Ask someone else to listen to the recording and to pick out what they think are the highlights. It's ideal to have a trusted friend or colleague go through the recording as what may seem insignificant and just 'what you do' to you may be the 'special' abilities that you have. You don't have to think about using these skills so you will have lots of headspace available to consider why they are seen as your 'special' abilities, whilst you just keep on living and doing you.

Take some time to look within and consider these super special abilities, how they can be brought to the forefront and best put to work for you. You can begin researching, reading and learning more about how to develop or fine-tune your abilities and then put these into practice.

You are unique and your super special abilities are what give you the X-factor in your life. Be unapologetically you.

'Be yourself. Everyone else is taken.'

Oscar Wilde.

TOP TIPS

➤ Consider your life story. Make a note of the accomplishments you have made.

➤ Record yourself talking about how you achieved each thing. Then listen to it and pick out your significant abilities and skills.

➤ Ask someone else to listen to the recording and pick out what they think your main skills are.

➤ Research and learn how best you can put these 'special' abilities into practice.

➤ Just do it!

Y – YOU FIRST

This chapter will help you if you:

➤ Want to know the importance of putting yourself first

➤ Want to know how to nourish yourself

➤ Want top tips on how to practise self-care.

'Every one of us needs to show how much we care for each other and, in the process, care for ourselves.'

Princess Diana.

What's the best investment you will ever make?

Take some time and really think about it before you read on.

The best investment you will ever make is in yourself! And in your wellness.

To those of you reading this book, this is a no brainer; but it's often a radical idea to others.

You can either choose to invest in your wellness or you may be forced to make time for your illness. Quite a disconcerting thought when you put it like this.

But here's the thing: no one is going to force you to care for yourself – it is all on you. You get to choose.

This is why it is so important to put yourself first and practise self-care.

Self-care is not an overindulgence. It is self-respect! And you are worth it. It is crucial for your wellness and success. Consistent actions become well-practised and eventually turn into habits and behaviours. Make them a priority if you want to be good at it.

So what does self-care mean to you?

Self-care has become an 'on trend' topic; it is plugged as something to resort to once you are exhausted and in need of solace from the relentlessness of life, often from the 'sleep when you're dead' brigade. It is posited as long bubble baths, indulgent desserts or a mani-pedi to escape the mundanities of life. Self-care isn't just about 'treating yourself', though, except for one caveat – rewards should be part of the accomplishment of your goals/intentions.

However, true self-care is not an escape. It is choosing you, choosing a lifestyle that is in line with supporting your needs – and being well. True self-care are the actions you take consistently to maintain your wellness. It is about managing yourself and making choices. Self-care is all about giving to yourself to create something better and to support the natural processes that should be prevalent in your life.

Sometimes this may mean doing things that are not at the top of your 'wants' list but are at the top of your 'needs' list. Sometimes it means reflecting upon failures and reviewing and regrouping to move forward with revised intentions. Sometimes it means forgoing the immediate satisfaction for the longer-term good. Sometimes it means letting go to move on. Sometimes it is doing things that are not 'mainstream' so you can live the way you want. Sometimes it is realising that the life portrayed in the media, movies and social media isn't real life and that it is okay to have washing-up in the sink or to not keep up with the 'latest faddy trends'.

Repeatedly, you may hear yourself saying, 'I don't have time for this' and it is one of the main obstacles people perceive when it comes to self-care. This may be controversial but the likelihood is that you do have the time; it is just a matter of prioritising. There are 1440 minutes in every day so your excuse for not finding 10 of these doesn't hold up (see Chapter L – Lifestyle).

Everyday life should be about choosing to be the hero of you, being honest with yourself and caring for your needs and not being the victim of your inner self-saboteur. If you are not taking care of yourself, then your life is out of balance.

Life does get busy between the home, family, walking the dog, work demands, you name it, and you're probably doing all of it. But implementing strategies to create a little more balance helps.

Consider that you are responsible for yourself and your self-care. You're on crowd control, damage limitation and maintenance work! Not only does this promote and reinforce positive habits and behaviours, improving your wellness and mindset, but it also helps keep issues at bay and supports restoration and recovery.

Giving back to your body, mind and soul is of über importance. You can get too caught up with the dos and don'ts. So, here are three simple things you can implement today as huge forms of self-care that will have a cumulative effect upon your wellness!

Let's take a look at the three principles of self-care and some easy-to-action solutions that you can implement today! Plus, there's a little bonus freebie for you!

The three principles of self-care are:
Nourish your body by giving it the nutrients it needs for energy, growth and restoration.

> ➤ Ensure that what you consume is nutrient-dense. Think local, seasonal, pastured and organic.

> ➤ Ensure you have adequate minerals. I highly recommend fulvic acid for this. It contains all the minerals you need that are deficient in the food chain.

> ➤ Ensure you are drinking quality water – not tap water! Also, all water is not equal. It may be H2O, but take a look at the work of Masuro Emoto on how the structure of water changes through what it's exposed to … powerful stuff.

Nourish your mind by being mindful or careful about what you allow to enter it!

> ➤ Ensure you are aware of your thoughts. They create your reality.

> ➤ Ensure you are giving the brain a workout. Aim to learn a new thing every day or to read. If you don't use your cognitive function, you lose it!

> ➤ Monitor your environment. Surround yourself with people, places and things that inspire you. They create positive emotions and you will perform better!

Nourish your soul by remembering that your soul or your ethereal body is your 'human energy field'. This can extend out about two metres!

> Ensure you are in control of your breathing. Yep, I know you do it, but calm breathing can support you in so many ways. My recommendations are nasal breaths and breathing into the diaphragm: place one hand on your chest and the other on your abdomen. As you breathe in, imagine there is a balloon in your tummy and you want to inflate this balloon by 360 degrees. The hand on the abdomen should rise before the hand on the chest.

> Ensure that you are grounded. The easiest way to do this is to get outside, barefoot on the ground, and recharge your battery from the earth!

> Ensure that you do the things that bring you joy. It's the feeling you get from happiness and pleasure, and it literally energises your soul!

Remember, self-care is important – nobody loves you as you should.

'Self-care isn't selfish. It's self-esteem.'

Ashley Judd.

TOP TIPS

> Take a moment now to write down three things you can do, one from each principle – mind, body and soul – that you can implement today as part of your self-care practice and for the next 30 days. You will be amazed at the impact this will have on your overall wellness and productivity.

> It's helpful to write these down and check them off daily.

> Aim to complete each of these 80% of the time to support your success (see Chapter L – Lifestyle for the 80% rule).

Z – ZZZZ: SLEEP

This chapter will help you if you:

➤ Want to know the importance of sleep

➤ Want to know what affects sleep

➤ Want top tips on how to practise good sleep hygiene.

Sleep is essential. It allows your body and mind to recharge and provides space for your soul to move into higher consciousness. It is a vital factor in nourishing your body, mind and soul.

Let's see why it truly is so important, including the benefits of having sleep, the effect of not getting enough sleep and the best ways to support your sleep hygiene for your wellness and to thrive.

Adequate sleep should leave you feeling refreshed and alert upon waking (when your cortisol is at its highest). You know how it feels when you don't have enough sleep – you feel groggy, can't think straight and often reach for the coffee before anything else.

Sleep is necessary for cognitive functions like learning, creativity, making decisions and remembering things. Sleep also helps you to manage your weight, support your immune system and regulate your hormones and emotions. It helps you to recover physically, maintain muscle mass and endurance, replenishes your energy and increases productivity. Your body heals and resets overnight.

Without sufficient sleep, these things all seem more difficult to do. Life becomes a grind.

You will spend approximately one-third of your life sleeping; however, in the UK, around a third of adults only manage five hours or less per night. Does this sound like you?

The sleep–wake body rhythm determines your need for sleep known as your sleep drive, which builds throughout the day and indicates to the body it requires sleep. The drive gets stronger the longer you are awake and is lowest after a full night's sleep. Your sleep runs in cycles that are approximately 90 minutes in duration and on average you'll have 4–5 cycles per night, so 5 cycles are 7 hours of sleep. Our body loves rhythms and consistency from which it starts to thrive.

If your sleep is interrupted or shortened, leptin production decreases and ghrelin production increases; this reduces the feeling of satiety and increases your hunger. Therefore, if disrupted for long periods, sleep has a direct impact upon your food consumption. In England, 28% of adults are obese and a further 36% are overweight. So there are clear associations between a lack of sleep and obesity.

Chronotype refers to our sleeping habits with the two main ones being morning and evening, or larks and owls. Larks are early risers, like to be active in the mornings, and have energy slumps in the afternoon. This accounts for around 50–60% of the population. Owls go to sleep late, have difficulty waking in the morning but have the highest activity in the afternoon and evening. This accounts for around 2–6% of the population. The remaining 34–48% fall somewhere in between.

It is interesting to know your chronotype as it allows you to better plan your days and indicates the time you are first able to fall asleep easily, relative to the time of onset of melatonin secretion. You can complete salivary tests to more accurately indicate onset, though completing an Automated Morningness-Eveningness Questionnaire to test your chronotype provides a good indication.

Do you find you are still tired when you wake; that you have low energy; you need to be fuelled by caffeine or, worse, energy drinks; you feel 'wired and tired'; struggle with your weight; have 'hormonal' issues; seem to have colds all the time; or are regularly injured from your workouts?

Then you need to sleep!

During sleep, your cells undergo periods of renewal and growth. Some are replaced and some are recycled; this supports replenishment and restoration. These processes are governed by your circadian rhythms (see Chapter C – Circadian rhythms).

This process affects your melatonin levels, which are naturally low when you wake, gradually increase throughout the morning and more rapidly from midday and peak around midnight. When this rhythm is in sync, melatonin supports hormone production (see Chapter H – Hormones) and acts as an antioxidant (see Chapter A – Antioxidants).

If you've had nights where you toss and turn and just cannot seem to drift off to sleep, this can impact the quality of your sleep and, sub-sequently, the quality of your day, whether it be from overthinking, feeling stressed or just not being able to get comfortable. In contrast, when you have restful sleep, then you're likely to enjoy your day to its fullest, have less tension and perform well.

When you are stressed, your sleep is affected – but have you ever con-sidered why? The pineal gland that secretes melatonin is really sensitive to adrenaline so the more stressed you are, particularly over extended periods, the more adrenaline you produce, which has a negative impact on melatonin production and hence your sleep! And when you don't sleep, you seem to overthink and become more anxious, which increases your stress. When you have internal stress, this elevates your need for energy and hence oxidation, which also increases the production of free radicals and the need for antioxidants (see Chapter A – Antioxidants). Seems like a catch-22.

This is not serving you. Next time you are facing a time where your stress levels are increased, try some of the techniques in the M – Mindfulness and U – Unwind chapters. To down-regulate your sympathetic nervous system and activate your parasympathetic nervous system, promote relaxation.

Becoming stressed about not sleeping is common but fuels the cycle and it won't help you to sleep. The important thing to note when you are applying strategies to enhance sleep is that it is simple, and consistency is key, so often doing small things over time has the biggest impact.

Developing good sleep hygiene is the key to quality sleep, though start with adding one factor into your life and being consistent, then gradually add in more.

TOP TIPS

➤ Test your chronotype to support planning your day optimally (see bibliography).

➤ Unplug. Avoid tech and screens 60 minutes before bed. This reduces stimulus, artificial light and sympathetic nervous system activation (see Chapter C – Circadian rhythms).

➤ Stop eating and drinking two to three hours before going to bed to ensure digestion is complete.

➤ Complete a journal/brain dump/daily review/to-do list before bed. It gets the info out of your head to reduce overthinking.

➤ Wake at the same time every day and develop a morning routine. Use a Lumie light or similar product to manipulate sunrise/sunset times and support sleep–awake cycles.

➤ Listen to binaural beats/solfeggio tines/calming music leading up to bedtime to relax your body and mind.

➤ Use transdermal magnesium oil on the soles of your feet, which has a calming and relaxing effect.

➤ If you're a caffeine junkie, try to avoid it after 2 pm.

➤ Move more during the day. This supports the need to sleep for rest.

➤ Sleep in a room that is completely dark. Only in pitch black does the body fully relax.

You are surrounded by stressors, some of them unseen, that are affecting your wellness. The main things to consider are sleep, hydration, movement, nutrition, environment and lifestyle choices.

But here's a secret: the most complex of tasks can become substantially easier and much simpler if you take them on one step at a time.

I truly hope that you find this book useful in making inroads towards improving your wellness. You've taken the first step already by investing in learning how best to support yourself and looking to be in a better place than you are at present. Now put these things into action, make them your daily practices and your sustainable habits.

If you are interested in further insights, then come and join other wellness seekers who have made a conscious decision to enjoy a space with a regular stream of support, tips and educational topics in order to enhance their wellness and find more ways to support themselves and their families.

Get on the list and be the first to know about things – sign up here – http://bit.ly/HTme

Love + Wellness

Tracy

BIBLIOGRAPHY

A – Antioxidants

➤ Mendelson, 2008. 10 – Nutritional Supplements and Metabolic Syndrome, https://www.sciencedirect.com/science/article/pii/B97801237424 07500127

➤ Mocchegiani & Straub, 2004. Possible New Anti-Ageing Strategies Related to Neuroendocrine-Immune Interactions, https://www.sciencedirect. com/science/article/abs/pii/S1567744304800279

➤ Reiter *et al.*, 2020. Melatonin in Mitochondria: Mitigating Clear and Present Dangers, https://doi.org/10.1152/physiol.00034.2019

➤ Spiegelberg, 2016. Humic and Fulvic Substances: A Reference Guide to Clinical Studies

➤ Ventura *et al.*, 2017. Selenium and Thyroid Disease: From Pathophysiology to Treatment, https://www.ncbi.nlm.nih.gov/pmc/articles/PMC 5307254/

B – Breathing

➤ Allen, 2015. The Health Benefits of Nose Breathing, https://www.lenus. ie/handle/10147/559021

➤ Dolan, https://www.breathguru.com/

➤ Gerritsen & Band, 2018. Breath of Life: The Respiratory Vagal Stimulation Model of Contemplative Activity, https://www.ncbi.nlm.nih.gov/pmc/articles/PMC6189422/

➤ Martarelli *et al.*, 2011. Diaphragmatic Breathing Reduces Exercise-Induced Oxidative Stress, https://www.ncbi.nlm.nih.gov/pmc/articles/PMC3139518/

➤ Pereira Pinto de Mendonça *et al.*, 2021. Buteyko Method for People with Asthma: A Protocol for a Systematic Review and Meta-Analysis, https://www.ncbi.nlm.nih.gov/pmc/articles/PMC8524279/

➤ Recinto *et al.*, 2017. Effects of Nasal or Oral Breathing on Anaerobic Power Output and Metabolic Responses, https://www.ncbi.nlm.nih.gov/pmc/articles/PMC5466403/

➤ Svenson *et al.*, 2006. Increased Net Water Loss by Oral Compared to Nasal Expiration in Healthy Subjects, https://pubmed.ncbi.nlm.nih.gov/16550955/

➤ Tamkin, 2020. Impact of Airway Dysfunction on Dental Health, https://www.ncbi.nlm.nih.gov/pmc/articles/PMC6986941/

➤ Telles *et al.*, 1994. Breathing through a Particular Nostril Can Alter Metabolism and Autonomic Activities, https://ijpp.com/IJPP%20archives/1994_38_2/133-137.pdf

C – Circadian rhythm

➤ Light temperature

➤ The Kelvin Temperature Scale

➤ Iris

➤ Blue blocking glasses

D – Detoxing

➤ Bókkan *et al.*, 2010. Picture Representation during REM Dreams: A Redox Molecular Hypothesis, https://pubmed.ncbi.nlm.nih.gov/20132862/

➤ Liver: Anatomy and Functions, https://www.hopkinsmedicine.org/health/conditions-and-diseases/liver-anatomy-and-functions

➤ https://hybridtherapy.thegoodinside.com/shop/product/super-green-juice

E – Energy/frequencies

- Bourzac, 2007. Lightning Bolts within Cells – A New Nanoscale Tool Reveals Strong Electric Fields inside Cells, https://www.technologyreview.com/2007/12/10/128544/lightning-bolts-within-cells/

- Eagleson *et al.*, 2016. The Power of Positive Thinking: Pathological Worry Is Reduced by Thought Replacement in Generalized Anxiety Disorder, https://www.ncbi.nlm.nih.gov/pmc/articles/PMC4760272/

- Håkansson *et al.*, 1994. Resonance Frequencies of the Human Skull in Vivo, https://www.researchgate.net/publication/15023312_Resonance_frequencies_of_the_human_skull_in_vivo

- Jepson, 2013. https://www.symmetrymagazine.org/article/july-2013/real-talk-everything-is-made-of-fields

- Lusak *et al*, 2022. Neurons Learn by Predicting Future Activity, https://www.nature.com/articles/s42256-021-00430-y

- Rahm *et al.*, 2017. Measuring the Frequency of Emotions— Validation of the Scale of Positive and Negative Experience (SPANE) in Germany, https://www.ncbi.nlm.nih.gov/pmc/articles/PMC5298234/

- Hamlaoui, 2020. The Human Body Frequency, https://www.researchgate.net/publication/340232697_The_human_body_frequency

- https://www.researchgate.net/publication/325090525_A_Primer_on_Energy_Frequencies_and_its_Use_Understanding_the_uses_and_benefits_of_energy_frequency_applications/link/5af5a5a00f7e9b026bcea98d/download

- Rogers *et al.*, 2021. Energy Healing Therapies: A Systematic Review and Critical Appraisal, https://www.researchgate.net/publication/349039163_Energy_Healing_Therapies_A_Systematic_Review_and_Critical_Appraisal

- Schneider & Cooper, 2019. A Brief History of the Chakras in Human Body, https://www.researchgate.net/publication/342562977_A_Brief_History_of_the_Chakras_in_Human_Body?channel=doi&linkId=5efb5246299bf18816f398d2&showFulltext=true

- Tseng *et al.*, 2014. The Frequency Preference of Neurons and Synapses in a Recurrent Oscillatory Network, https://www.researchgate.net/publication/265792291_The_Frequency_Preference_of_Neurons_and_Synapses_in_a_Recurrent_Oscillatory_Network

➤ Von Bartheld *et al.*, 2016. The Search for True Numbers of Neurons and Glial Cells in the Human Brain: A Review of 150 Years of Cell Counting, https://www.ncbi.nlm.nih.gov/pmc/articles/PMC5063692/pdf/nihms799882.pdf

F – Failing

➤ https://www.merriam-webster.com/dictionary/failing%20that

G – Grounding

➤ Chevalier *et al.*, 2012. Earthing: Health Implications of Reconnecting the Human Body to the Earth's Surface Electron, https://www.ncbi.nlm.nih.gov/pmc/articles/PMC3265077/pdf/JEPH2012-291541.pdf

➤ Chevalier *et al.*, 2013. Earthing (Grounding) the Human Body Reduces Blood Viscosity—a Major Factor in Cardiovascular Disease, https://www.ncbi.nlm.nih.gov/pmc/articles/PMC3576907/

➤ Earthing Movie, bit.ly/EarthingMovieYouTube

➤ Earth Runners, https://earthrunners.com/?rfsn=6509063.e348bb

➤ Grounding Mat: https://www.amazon.co.uk/s?k=grounding+mat&dc&crid=3RUYOHGGTWLJF&qid=1643285142&sprefix=grounding+mat%2Cstripbooks%2C67&ref=sr_ex_n_0

➤ Menigoz *et al.*, 2020. Integrative and Lifestyle Medicine Strategies Should Include Earthing (Grounding): Review of Research Evidence and Clinical Observations, https://reader.elsevier.com/reader/sd/pii/S1550830719305476?token=72CD8D78BD8D2AE125646DDDEE54AFCB45FC2229D66BB5C139344E794514DD7ED91978CF96E6686F92D5411CCD52F125&originRegion=eu-west-1&originCreation=20211222151232

➤ Oschman *et al.*, 2015. The Effects of Grounding (Earthing) on Inflammation, the Immune Response, Wound Healing, and Prevention and Treatment of Chronic Inflammatory and Autoimmune Diseases, https://www.ncbi.nlm.nih.gov/pmc/articles/PMC4378297/pdf/jir-8-083.pdf

➤ Sinatra *et al.*, 2017. Electric Nutrition: The Surprising Health and Healing Benefits of Biological Grounding (Earthing). Alternative Therapies in Health and Medicine, 23(5): 8–16

H – Hormones

➤ Biosignature Modulation, https://drbillsukala.com/spot-reduction-bio signature-modulation/

➤ Colpo, A. The Great Cholesterol Con

➤ Dunn, 2000. Trace Element and Mineral Nutrition in Endocrine Diseases, https://www.researchgate.net/publication/302162658_Trace_Element_ and_Mineral_Nutrition_in_Endocrine_Diseases

➤ DUTCH Test, https://regeneruslabs.com/products/dutch-sex-hormone-metabolism

➤ Krause & Cohen, 2014. Not All Brains Are Created Equal: The Relevance of Individual Differences in Responsiveness to Transcranial Electrical Stimulation. Frontiers in Systems Neuroscience, 8(25).

➤ Petrenko *et al.*, 2017. Analysis of the Functional State of Students in the Process of Healthy Training Exercises in Different Phases of the Ovarian-Menstrual Cycle. Pedagogics, Psychology, Medical Biological Problems of Physical Training and Sports, 21(6) pp. 285–290

➤ Salivary Cortisol, https://regeneruslabs.com/products/diurnal-cortisol-5

➤ Yokoyama S, *et al.*, 1994. Combined Effects of Magnesium Deficiency and an Atherogenic Level of Low Density Lipoprotein on Uptake and Metabo-lism of Low Density Lipoprotein by Cultured Human Endothelial Cells. II. Electron Microscopic Data. Magnes Res., 7(2) pp. 97–105 https:// pubmed.ncbi.nlm.nih.gov/7999534/

I – Intentions

➤ Chopra, 2020. 5 Steps to Setting Powerful Intentions, https://chopra. com/articles/5-steps-to-setting-powerful-intentions

J – Journalling

➤ Reece, 2014. Journalling, https://www.researchgate.net/publication/ 277670430_Journalling

K – Kindness

➤ https://www.brucelipton.com/

➤ https://www.brucelipton.com/resource/article/the-wisdom-your-cells

L – Lifestyle

➤ Christiensen & Matuska, 2011, Lifestyle Balance: A Review of Concepts and Research, https://www.tandfonline.com/doi/abs/10.1080/1442759 1.2006.9686570

➤ Veal, 1993. The Concept of Lifestyle: A Review, https://www.research-gate.net/publication/248996076_The_Concept_of_Lifestyle_A_ Review

➤ Kinkhabwala & Gor, 2018. Transcending from a Healthy Life to a Holistic Living – Role of Spirituality, https://www.researchgate.net/ publication/316105890_Transcending_From_a_Healthy_Life_to_a_ Holistic_Living_-_Role_of_Spirituality

➤ Pronk *et al.*, 2010. The Association between Optimal Lifestyle Adherence and Short-Term Incidence of Chronic Conditions among Employees, https://www.researchgate.net/publication/49622293_The_Association_ Between_Optimal_Lifestyle_Adherence_and_Short-Term_Incidence_of_ Chronic_Conditions_among_Employees

M – Movement

➤ Raichlen *et al.*, 2017. Physical Activity Patterns and Biomarkers of Cardio-vascular Disease Risk in Hunter-Gatherers, https://pubmed.ncbi.nlm.nih.gov/27723159/

➤ Gabbard, 2009. Optimizing Brain and Motor Development through Movement. https://www.researchgate.net/publication/236512418_Opti-mizing_brain_and_motor_development_through_movement

N – Nutrients

➤ Check, 2018. How to Eat, Move and Be Healthy.

➤ Ghosal, 2006. Shilajit in Perspective. Narosa Publishing House, Oxford, UK.

➤ Kang & Choi, 2009. Oxidative Degradation of Organic Compounds Using Zero-Valent Iron in the Presence of Natural Organic Matter Serving as an Electron Shuttle, https://pubs.acs.org/doi/pdf/10.1021/es801705f

➤ Dr J. Tennant Interview with Dr Mercola, https://fb.watch/ahBcJCX29Y/

➤ Cell Energy and Cell Functions, https://www.nature.com/scitable/ topicpage/cell-energy-and-cell-functions-14024533/

O – Oils

➤ Ali *et al.*, 2015. Essential Oils Used in Aromatherapy: A Systemic Review, https://www.sciencedirect.com/sdfe/reader/pii/S2221169115001033/pdf

➤ A Brief History of Aromatherapy, http://ultranl.com/wp-content/uploads/Aromatherapy_History.pdf

➤ Farrar & Farrar, 2020. Clinical Aromatherapy, https://www.ncbi.nlm.nih.gov/pmc/articles/PMC7520654/pdf/main.pdf

➤ IFA. Safety and Toxicology, https://ifaroma.org/en_GB/home/explore_aromatherapy/safety

➤ Worwood, Valerie Ann. (1991). The Complete Book of Essential Oils and Aromatherapy

P – Presence

➤ Carmody & Baer, 2008. Relationships between Mindfulness Practise and Levels of Mindfulness, Medical and Psychological Symptoms and Well-being in a Mindfulness-Based Stress Reduction Program, https://pubmed.ncbi.nlm.nih.gov/17899351/

➤ Evans *et al.*, 2009. The Effects of Mindfulness and Self-Consciousness on Persistence, https://www.sciencedirect.com/science/article/abs/pii/S0191886909001421

➤ Keng *et al.*, 2011. Effects of Mindfulness on Psychological Health: A Review of Empirical Studies, https://www.ncbi.nlm.nih.gov/pmc/articles/PMC3679190/

Q – Quality over quantity

➤ Canfield, https://www.jackcanfield.com/blog/using-the-law-of-attraction/

➤ Liu & Baskin (2020). The Quality Versus Quantity Trade-Off: Why and When Choices for Self Versus Others Differ, https://journals.sagepub.com/doi/epub/10.1177/0146167220941677

R – Resilience

➤ Luthar *et al.* 2014. Resilience and Positive Psychology, https://www.researchgate.net/profile/Suniya-Luthar/publication/286526146_Resilience_and_Positive_Psychology/links/56719bca08aed8f3115cd68c/Resilience-and-Positive-Psychology.pdf

S – Sunshine

➤ D-Minder App, https://dminder.ontometrics.com/

➤ Hamblin, 2017. Ultraviolet Irradiation of Blood: 'The Cure That Time Forgot'?, https://www.ncbi.nlm.nih.gov/pmc/articles/PMC6122858/pdf/nihms-986489.pdf

➤ Hart & Norval, 2021. More Than Effects in Skin: Ultraviolet Radiation-Induced Changes in Immune Cells in Human Blood, https://www.frontiersin.org/articles/10.3389/fimmu.2021.694086/full

➤ Vitamin D Test, https://www.vitamindtest.org.uk/

➤ Wacker & Holick, 2013, Sunlight and Vitamin D – A Global Perspective for Health, https://www.ncbi.nlm.nih.gov/pmc/articles/PMC3897598/pdf/de-5-51.pdf

T – Thoughts

➤ Electromagnetic Theories of Consciousness, https://en.wikipedia.org/wiki/Electromagnetic_theories_of_consciousness

➤ How Much Energy Does the Brain Use?, https://www.brainfacts.org/brain-anatomy-and-function/anatomy/2019/how-much-energy-does-the-brain-use

➤ Steimer, 2002. The Biology of Fear – and Anxiety-Related Behaviours, https://www.ncbi.nlm.nih.gov/pmc/articles/PMC3181681/pdf/DialoguesClinNeurosci-4-231.pdf

U – Unwind

➤ Bordoni *et al.*, 2018. The Anatomical Relationships of the Tongue with the Body System, https://www.ncbi.nlm.nih.gov/pmc/articles/PMC6390887/#:~:text=The%20tongue%20position%20influences%20the,reduce%20its%20activity%20%20%5B17%5D.

➤ Schmidt *et al.*, 2009. Effects of Tongue Position on Mandibular Muscle Activity and Heart Rate Function, https://pubmed.ncbi.nlm.nih.gov/19773187/

➤ Why Your Brain Needs More Downtime, https://www.scientificamerican.com/article/mental-downtime/

V – Visualisation

➤ Blackwell, 2018. Mental Imagery: From Basic Research to Clinical Practice, https://www.researchgate.net/publication/322650794_Mental_Imagery_From_Basic_Research_to_Clinical_Practice

➤ Cumming & Williams, 2012. The Role of Imagery in Performance, https://www.researchgate.net/publication/267749244_The_Role_of_Imagery_in_Performance

➤ Dispenza, 2012. Breaking the Habit of Being Yourself. Hay House

W – Water

➤ Gibbens, 2019. Exposed to Extreme Heat, Plastic Bottles May Ultimately Become Unsafe, https://www.nationalgeographic.co.uk/environment-and-conservation/2019/07/exposed-extreme-heat-plastic-bottles-may-ultimately-become

➤ Horton *et al.*, 2018. *Giardia Duodenalis* in the UK: Current Knowledge of Risk Factors and Public Health Implications, https://www.cambridge.org/core/journals/parasitology/article/giardia-duodenalis-in-the-uk-current-knowledge-of-risk-factors-and-public-health-implications/38EDAF34153591775E1163C9B579986C

➤ Oakley & Baird, 2015. Do Patients Drink Enough Water? Actual Pure Water Intake Compared to the Theoretical Daily Rules of Drinking Eight 8-Ounce Glasses and Drinking Half Your Body Weight in Ounces, http://dx.doi.org/10.4236/jwarp.2015.711072

➤ Pollack, 2013. The Fourth Phase of Water: Beyond Solid, Liquid, and Vapor. Ebner and Sons Publishers

➤ Popkin *et al.*, 2010. Water, Hydration and Health, https://www.ncbi.nlm.nih.gov/pmc/articles/PMC2908954/

➤ Sokol, 2019. Black, Hot Ice May Be Nature's Most Common Form of Water, https://www.quantamagazine.org/black-hot-superionic-ice-may-be-natures-most-common-form-of-water-20190508/?fbclid=IwAR0YNVA1EIUN64Bh-B2OZ55Uzh9EQBTJDSycMNIMrn42CXg63PEU6Uynvcg

X – X-factor

➤ Burrow & Rainone, 2016. How Many Likes Did I Get?: Purpose Moderates Links between Positive Social Media Feedback and Self-Esteem, https://www.researchgate.net/publication/308184561_How_many_

likes_did_I_get_Purpose_moderates_links_between_positive_social_media_feedback_and_self-esteem

➢ Hill *et al.*, 2016. The Value of a Purposeful Life: Sense of Purpose Predicts Greater Income and Net Worth, https://www.ncbi.nlm.nih.gov/pmc/articles/PMC5408461/

➢ Hill *et al.*, 2018. Sense of Purpose Moderates the Associations between Daily Stressors and Daily Well-Being, http://midus.wisc.edu/findings/pdfs/1762.pdf

Y – You first

➢ Godfrey *et al.*, 2010. The Experience of Self-care: A Systematic Review, https://pubmed.ncbi.nlm.nih.gov/27819888/

➢ Narasimhan *et al.*, 2019. Self-Care Interventions to Advance Health and Wellbeing: A Conceptual Framework to Inform Normative Guidance, https://www.bmj.com/content/365/bmj.l688

➢ Riegel *et al.*, 2021. Self-Care Research: Where Are We Now? Where Are We Going?, https://www.sciencedirect.com/science/article/pii/S0020748919302093

Z – Zzzz: sleep

➢ Aminoff *et al.*, 2011. We Spend About One-Third of Our Life Either Sleeping or Attempting To Do So, https://pubmed.ncbi.nlm.nih.gov/21056174/

➢ Cooper *et al.*, 2018. Sleep Deprivation and Obesity in Adults: A Brief Narrative Review, https://bmjopensem.bmj.com/content/4/1/e000392

➢ Horne & Östberg, 1976. A Self-Assessment Questionnaire to Determine Morningness-Eveningness in Human Circadian Rhythms, https://pubmed.ncbi.nlm.nih.gov/1027738/

➢ Kloss *et al.*, 2015. Sleep, Sleep Disturbance and Fertility in Women, https://www.ncbi.nlm.nih.gov/pmc/articles/PMC4402098/#R8

➢ Lin *et al.*, 2013. Somatic Symptoms, Psychological Distress and Sleep Disturbance among Infertile Women with Intrauterine Insemination Treatment, https://pubmed.ncbi.nlm.nih.gov/23829562/

➢ López-Muñoz *et al.*, 2016. Melatonin Neuroprotective Agents and Antidepressant Therapy.

➤ Obesity Statistics, https://commonslibrary.parliament.uk/research-brief ings/sn03336/

➤ Sleepless Cities Revealed as One in Three Adults Suffer from Insomnia, 2017, https://www.aviva.com/newsroom/news-releases/2017/10/Sleepless-cities-revealed-as-one-in-three-adults-suffer-from-insomnia/

➤ Taking Sleep Seriously, 2020, https://www.mentalhealth.org.uk/sites/default/files/MHF_Sleep_Report_UK.pdf

➤ Test Your Chronotype, https://chronotype-self-test.info/index.php

THE AUTHOR

Tracy Richardson is a holistic sports therapist (MSc.), a holistic health coach and educator (QTLS) who utilises a variety of modalities to support health-conscious people to reduce pain, renew energy & restore wellness.

With a background that includes fitness, healthcare, wellness, education, sports and holistic therapy, she has a wealth of knowledge and experiences to draw upon, facilitating and supporting others along their wellness journey.

When not working, you can find her walking her dog, spending time with friends and family, or geeking out studying about the body and its inner workings – from cellular energy to the influence of the universe.

Based in Warwickshire, England, she is a huge advocate for self-care as the best investment you will ever make into your wellness. You can find Tracy online providing a regular stream of support, tips and educational topics to gain insight and enhance wellness.

If you would like more information on the services Tracy offers and her approach to client wellness, please visit: www.hybridtherapy.uk

Get on the list to receive regular updates and be the first to know about things – sign up here – http://bit.ly/HTme.